The Group

The Group

*Seven Widowed Fathers
Reimagine Life*

BY DONALD L. ROSENSTEIN, MD

JUSTIN M. YOPP, PHD

OXFORD
UNIVERSITY PRESS

OXFORD
UNIVERSITY PRESS

Oxford University Press is a department of the University of Oxford. It furthers
the University's objective of excellence in research, scholarship, and education
by publishing worldwide. Oxford is a registered trade mark of Oxford University
Press in the UK and certain other countries.

Published in the United States of America by Oxford University Press
198 Madison Avenue, New York, NY 10016, United States of America.

Library of Congress Cataloging-in-Publication Data
Names: Rosenstein, Donald, author. | Yopp, Justin M., author.
Title: The group : seven widowed fathers reimagine life /
by Donald L. Rosenstein, MD, Justin M. Yopp, PhD.
Description: New York, NY, United States of America : Oxford University Press, [2018] |
Includes bibliographical references. Identifiers: LCCN 2017007216 |
ISBN 9780190649562 (hardback)
Subjects: LCSH: Bereavement—Psychological aspects. | Widowers—Psychology. |
Fathers—Psychology.
Classification: LCC BF575.G7 R677 2018 | DDC 155.9/3708655—dc23
LC record available at https://lccn.loc.gov/2017007216

This material is not intended to be, and should not be considered, a substitute for medical or other
professional advice. Treatment for the conditions described in this material is highly dependent on
the individual circumstances. And, while this material is designed to offer accurate information with
respect to the subject matter covered and to be current as of the time it was written, research and
knowledge about medical and health issues is constantly evolving and dose schedules for medications
are being revised continually, with new side effects recognized and accounted for regularly. Readers
must therefore always check the product information and clinical procedures with the most up-to-date
published product information and data sheets provided by the manufacturers and the most recent
codes of conduct and safety regulation. The publisher and the authors make no representations or
warranties to readers, express or implied, as to the accuracy or completeness of this material. Without
limiting the foregoing, the publisher and the authors make no representations or warranties as to the
accuracy or efficacy of the drug dosages mentioned in the material. The authors and the publisher do
not accept, and expressly disclaim, any responsibility for any liability, loss or risk that may be claimed
or incurred as a consequence of the use and/or application of any of the contents of this material.

9 8 7 6 5 4 3 2 1

Printed by Sheridan Books, Inc., United States of America

This book is dedicated to the memories of:
Deanna
Joy
Sarah
Kelley
Susan
Catie
Lisa

CONTENTS

Reunion, 2017: Standing (from left)—Bruce, Steve, Karl, Dan, Russ;
seated (from left)—Joe, Neill

PART I

Unimaginable Loss

Neill's Dilemma

"Dad, you *cannot* be serious!"

Julie had made what she thought was a simple request: Could she go to the hockey game with her friends on Friday night? To her father, Neill, it was a very big deal. That Friday would be the first anniversary of the death of his wife (Julie's mother), Deanna. Neill had spent weeks figuring out just the right way to mark the date, ultimately deciding to take his four children to visit the gravesite, release balloons, and then have dinner at what had been Deanna's favorite restaurant. Most importantly, they would spend the day together as a family, something Deanna would have liked. Now, with the anniversary only a week away, his fifteen-year-old daughter wanted out.

"Are you really saying that I can't go?" Julie asked again.

"That's exactly what I'm saying," Neill said tersely. "You do realize why next Friday is so important, right?" When he questioned whether she cared more about going to a hockey game than honoring her mother, Julie became indignant. She shot back that just because she wanted to hang out with her friends did not mean she had forgotten about Mom. The argument escalated quickly. Neill was resolute; like it or not, she would be spending next Friday night with her family. Julie stormed off to her room and slammed the door.

For the next several days, they barely spoke to each other. Neill could not believe his daughter was acting as if the first anniversary of her mother's death was just another day. Still, he hated that they were arguing. He knew that Julie was grieving too and he worried, not for the first time since Deanna died, that his initial reaction had been unnecessarily harsh. Neill felt lost and alone. As he had done from time to time over the past year, he lay down on his bed, looked up, and talked aloud to Deanna. But the one-way "conversation" brought little clarity.

The next night, Neill attended a support group for men who were widowed fathers raising children on their own. The two of us, a psychiatrist (Don) and a clinical psychologist (Justin), had recently formed the group and this was just the second time the fathers had met. Neill, a private man, had joined reluctantly. He never would have imagined discussing such personal details with people he barely knew. But with the anniversary only days away, and still at odds with Julie, he was desperate for guidance. He described his dilemma and looked to us—the "experts"—for advice. But at that point there were no studies and few theories to help resolve a problem like this, so we asked the group what they thought Neill should do.

The men immediately identified with Neill's situation and appreciated his instinct to hold his ground on something that was so important to him. Still, the last thing he needed was to be dragging a sullen teenager to the cemetery and out to dinner. The fathers' advice was unequivocal: "Let your daughter go to the hockey game." As a fifteen-year-old girl still adjusting to her mother's death, she probably needed the distraction. Wanting to hang out with friends on a Friday night is normal, and normalcy was probably something Julie was desperately craving. Besides, one of the fathers pointed out, not wanting to spend the anniversary in the way dictated by your father is not the same as being disrespectful of your mother's memory.

Had a friend or family member so directly challenged Neill's stance, he might have dismissed the advice as coming from someone who couldn't understand what he was going through. Hearing from others who were "in the same awful boat" was different. These guys *got it*, the whole widowed father thing. They suggested a compromise: Allow Julie to go out with her friends after visiting the cemetery as a family in the afternoon. That sounded reasonable enough to Neill and having a plan gave him the confidence to talk with Julie again.

The group discussion helped Neill in other ways too. With the anniversary of Deanna's death approaching, he had found himself ruminating about the end of her life. He had been replaying the medical decisions he was forced to make during her final days and he still wondered what he could have done differently. After being alone with his thoughts and feelings for so long, the meeting was the first time Neill shared with others all that he was going through. He left the meeting that evening feeling less burdened.

The next afternoon, Neill sat down with Julie. He said that he respected her right to grieve in her own way. He also explained why spending the day together as a family was important to him and he proposed the compromise. Julie listened quietly and without objection. Several days later, Neill and his four children visited the cemetery and remembered the wife and mother they had lost a year earlier. That evening, Julie went out with her friends. The anniversary had not unfolded as Neill had first imagined, but it turned out to be a meaningful day and the crisis with his daughter had passed.

Neill reported back to the other fathers at the next meeting. He thanked them for their help and admitted that asking for parenting advice had been difficult for him. Bruce, another father with a teenage daughter, quickly joked that Neill was not the only incompetent parent in the room. "I'm just glad you went first!" It was the group's first light moment as they acknowledged to each other that they were in way over their heads.

The discussion then turned to the upcoming holidays, which for most of the men would be the first without their wives. Bruce jumped in again: "I'm absolutely dreading Christmas. And now my youngest daughter says she wants to hang a stocking for her Mom. Honestly, that one had not even crossed my mind. Any thoughts, guys?"

■

As far as we could tell, a support group specifically for widowed fathers had never been done before. Our interest in starting one grew directly from our clinical experiences caring for patients and their families at the Lineberger Comprehensive Cancer Center at the University of North Carolina (UNC). In our roles at the cancer hospital, we often consult with patients nearing the end of their lives. Within the span of a few of months, we cared for several terminally ill women with young children at home. Their sadness was profound and the inevitability of leaving their children nearly too much for them to handle. Furthermore, their anxiety about how their husbands would manage without them was palpable.

Our thoughts remained with these families after the mothers died. We had met several of the fathers during their wives' treatment and could only imagine what it was like for them to assume all parenting responsibilities, including helping their children grieve, in the midst of their own mourning. As the sole caregiver in the home, each man felt an unavoidable need to carry on. We thought they would benefit from meeting with other widowed parents and assumed that we could refer them to existing support groups. Surprisingly, we were unable to find a single program specific to their needs, either locally or nationally. We soon realized that both clinicians and researchers had almost completely neglected the needs of widowed fathers.

We started the Single Fathers Due to Cancer Program to fill this gap. Seven fathers signed up for the original support group. Five of them— Karl, Bruce, Dan, Joe, and Neill—were present the night of the first meeting. Two others, Russ and Steve, would join later. Initially, we scheduled just six sessions. Instead, the men would meet regularly for nearly four years. Over that time, each father navigated his darkest days and began to reimagine a future for his children and himself. The fathers would become enthusiastic collaborators with us on educational and research projects and, in turn, bring much-needed attention to the challenges facing widowed parents. Each man has encouraged us to write this book, which grew directly from our work together.

■

Most of us carry a general expectation about how our lives will unfold. This may include finding someone to love and grow old with; working in a meaningful and fulfilling career; raising healthy and well-adjusted children; or establishing roots and a place to call home. But plans change or tragedy strikes and our life trajectories become disrupted in unpredictable ways.

Figuring out how to honor the first anniversary of your wife's death while managing both your and your children's grief is a challenge specific to widowed parents. However, on a fundamental level, it illustrates a phenomenon that nearly everyone faces at some point in their lives: how to adapt following a loss. Whereas the death of a loved one is perhaps the most profound example, loss comes in all forms. Being diagnosed with a serious illness. Ending a relationship. Suffering a life-altering injury. Learning that your child will face developmental delays. Surrendering your home to foreclosure. Being laid off from work. The manner in which Neill and the other fathers adapted to their new lives has relevance for people facing all types of loss.

On the whole, people are more resilient than they might imagine. Yet exactly *how* someone adapts following a major loss is not well understood. This book integrates the experiences of seven widowed fathers with contemporary research findings and, in doing so, provides a novel and up-to-date perspective on response to loss.

This book also illustrates the healing potential of shared grief. Perhaps more telling than their individual struggles is the shared story of seven men, brought together by tragic circumstances, who supported each other in ways no one else could. Over the course of several years, they encouraged each other through painful setbacks and celebrated increasingly frequent successes for both themselves and their children. In the end, each father benefited enormously by sharing with, and giving to, each other.

As facilitators of the group, we had the privilege of participating in the fathers' connection with and generosity toward each other. We developed a deep respect and fondness for these men who, like us, hope that this book will provide some measure of solace for those struggling to adapt to what may seem like an insurmountable loss. Their willingness to share their hard-earned insights and wisdom has informed and inspired us.

2

The First Meeting

Dan had been terrified of speaking in front of people for as long as he could remember. As a child, he avoided eye contact with teachers so they wouldn't call on him in class and he insisted on non-speaking parts when he had to participate in school plays. In high school, he feigned stomachaches to avoid giving class presentations and never dared to run for student council. Over time, Dan's fear of embarrassment shaped his personality. He was shy and introverted, and he stayed away from situations that invited scrutiny.

Naturally, when Dan first heard about a new support group for recently widowed fathers, he thought there was no way he could join. Opening up to a room full of strangers about his wife's illness and recent death was nightmare material. It was precisely the kind of situation he had spent a lifetime avoiding.

Still, Dan knew that he needed some kind of help. He had been in bad shape in the months since his wife had died. He felt isolated in his grief and overwhelmed by the prospect of raising two children by himself. As Dan saw it, his kids not only lost their mother but were now stuck with a father whose ineptitude as a parent was only making things worse: a cruel "double-whammy." Despite his fears, he decided to join the support group because he felt he owed it to his children to be a better parent.

Dan set the bar low for that first night: show up, sit quietly, listen to the other fathers, and avoid drawing attention to himself. If asked to share his story, he would offer only the barest of details. If called on to participate in group discussion, he would keep his input to a minimum.

As he pulled into the parking lot for the first meeting, Dan felt a familiar wave of anxiety. His stomach churned and his heart began to pound. He thought about turning back. Instead, Dan closed his eyes and tried to calm down. After ten minutes, he took a deep breath and stepped out of the car.

■

Dan was one of six fathers who attended the support group on that first night. Seated around an oval table in a nondescript clinic conference room, the only thing the men knew about one another was what they could infer from their attendance: that each had recently lost his spouse and had children at home. Some made small talk while waiting for the meeting to begin. Dan sat nervously and stared down at his phone, wishing he could be an observer rather than an active participant.

When the fathers had all arrived, we introduced ourselves as the facilitators of the group and explained that our clinical work and the lack of resources for widowed fathers had led us to start this project. We outlined our plans for the group: six monthly sessions, each focused on an aspect of being a widowed parent. Meetings would begin with a 30- to 45-minute lecture (for example, on how to tell the difference between normal grief and depression in a child) followed by group discussion. To make it easier for the men to attend, we arranged for child care in a room down the hall.

We then asked each father to introduce himself and share his story. This was the moment Dan feared most. As it turned out, each man found it painstakingly difficult to condense the story of his wife's diagnosis, treatment, and death and somehow articulate how he and his children were coping.

Karl, a computer software engineer and father of two, volunteered to go first. His wife had died earlier that year from lung cancer that had spread to her brain. Throughout her treatment, she stayed single-mindedly focused on finding a cure and opted for experimental chemotherapy when standard drugs failed to slow her cancer. In her final weeks, with her mental clarity failing, she was unable to say goodbye to either Karl or their children. Karl deeply regretted not having seen sooner that the end of his wife's life was near. "Even though I knew she was going to die, it all happened so fast at the end. It was too late before I realized it was too late."

Joe introduced himself next and spoke in a hushed, measured voice. His style was earnest and straightforward as he described his wife's five-year struggle with breast cancer. For Joe, adapting to single fatherhood included the challenge of parenting children at very different developmental stages. This was most striking when he talked with them about their mother's death. Conversations with his two oldest daughters, a junior and senior in high school, were candid and practical. In contrast, Joe used much simpler language with his youngest child, a daughter with Down syndrome who had just started kindergarten. The discussion with his eleven-year-old son required a different approach altogether.

Bruce seemed most at ease in the group setting as he chatted with the others before the meeting began. But his social gifts hardly made it easy for him to talk about losing his wife to colon cancer. Shaking his head and wiping away tears, he acknowledged that her death still felt unreal to him six months later. Being a widower in his mid-forties was not how his life was supposed to turn out. Shortly before she died, Bruce's wife told him that as a future single parent of their three daughters, he had it harder than she did. Having watched her endure months of grueling treatment, he dismissed the comment as absurd. Now, trying to raise his girls, work full-time, and manage a household on his own, Bruce wondered if his wife had been right after all.

Neill was already preparing for the first anniversary of Deanna's death, but it would not be until the next month's meeting—after his argument with his daughter—that he brought it up for group discussion. The previous autumn, Deanna had developed respiratory symptoms and was initially misdiagnosed. Without the appropriate treatment, her condition rapidly worsened and within weeks of her first, seemingly innocuous symptoms, Neill was a widowed father. In that way, his experience differed from the others: he hadn't watched his wife decline during a prolonged course of cancer treatment. But, just like the others, his grief was profound and his confidence in raising his children was deeply shaken.

The next father to speak was a young man who was stationed at a nearby military base, far from his extended family. His wife had died only weeks earlier, leaving him to raise three very young children. He described caring for his children during his wife's numerous and lengthy hospitalizations and he sobbed as he shared details of the day she died. This father would return the following month, but after that we never heard from him again. We suspected that either it was too soon after his wife's death to talk about it all or that the group format was too uncomfortable for him.

As the only person left to introduce himself, Dan had nowhere to hide. Another rush of anxiety swept over him as he began to describe his wife and how they had first met nearly twenty years earlier. He had recently moved to North Carolina and was attending a small election night party where a friend introduced him to Sarah. Although he was nervous at first, Dan's anxieties waned the more they talked. They had the same political views and soon discovered shared interests in literature, music, movies, and the outdoors.

Dan and Sarah dated for two years before getting married and starting a family. Dan worked as a reading specialist at a local high school, a rewarding job that allowed him to work individually with students and required no public speaking. Sarah started a company translating high-tech user manuals into foreign languages. At home, Dan instilled in their son and daughter his love for music and taught them how to find serenity in nature. He and Sarah were loving and attentive parents who prioritized family time with their two children above all else.

Each summer, the four of them visited Dan's side of the family in upstate New York. For Sarah, the vacation was a much anticipated break from the humidity of the South and a chance to unplug from work. So a nagging, upset stomach was not going to keep her from making the trip. She spent most of the week resting in bed but insisted it was just a bug. On the long drive back to North Carolina, Sarah was miserable. The pain in her abdomen was sharp and relentless. When they pulled over at a rest stop in Virginia, she noticed blood in her urine. Dan wanted to find the nearest emergency room, but Sarah insisted on getting home and going into work the next morning. By the next afternoon, with the pain having persisted, she relented. Dan rushed her to the hospital where she went through a series of scans and blood tests. The diagnosis was devastating: advanced-stage colon cancer that had already metastasized throughout her body.

Treatment started immediately and was all-consuming. Hospital admissions, doctors' appointments, and chemotherapy infusions book-ended stretches when Sarah was too exhausted to get out of bed. After five months, not only had her tumors failed to shrink, but, in the words of her oncologist, they had "spread like wildfire." Her healthcare team recommended hospice, but neither she nor Dan was ready. Sarah wanted desperately to live as long as she could; her children needed their Mom. But she was growing weaker and becoming less alert. One night, while Dan was helping her to the bathroom, her legs gave out and she fell to the ground. Hearing the fall, their daughter ran out of her bedroom and was distraught at the sight of her mother on the tile floor. The next morning, Dan called to arrange for home hospice.

The following week was a blur. Dan hosted family and friends who came to say goodbye to Sarah. He negotiated tasks with the hospice nurses and slept whenever he could. When he told his children that their mother was dying, they were not as surprised as he had anticipated. Dan never initiated a similar conversation with Sarah.

In the weeks following Sarah's death, Dan was inundated with help. Neighbors organized a schedule for home-cooked meals, friends volunteered to drive the children to after-school activities, and it seemed like everyone was checking in on him. Dan found the influx of visitors and the focus on his state of mind overwhelming. Still, the help was desperately needed. And then . . . it all stopped. The meals were no longer delivered and the offers to shuttle the children around town dried up. Soon, his freezer, which had once been full of ready-made meals from the "casserole brigade" was nearly empty. He and the children were suddenly on their own.

"It felt like I woke up one morning and it was all gone," Dan said as he finished introducing himself to the group. "It seems like everyone got back to their normal lives. And now, it's all on me." In the end, Dan spoke longer and offered more detail than he had expected. Nonetheless, he was relieved when his turn was over.

The rest of us sat in silence after Dan finished his story. As mental health professionals with years of clinical experience in cancer hospitals, we were accustomed to hearing about awful and seemingly insurmountable circumstances. Yet, the collective magnitude of the loss these men had experienced, coupled with what they were still facing, was staggering. Had this first meeting been too intense? The men were already struggling with their own grief; perhaps exposing them to one tragic story after another was precisely the *wrong* thing to do. At that moment, we wondered whether the first gathering of the Single Fathers Due to Cancer support group would also be the last.

One of us (Don) broke the silence by acknowledging how difficult the last forty minutes had been and said that the rest of the evening and subsequent meetings were not likely to be quite so intense. That said, each father would have to continue sharing painful details of his story. For this group to work, the men would have to take a collective leap of faith.

We asked the fathers why they joined the group. Some said they came at the urging of their friends and families. Several, including Dan, were drawn by the program's implied focus on parenting. Had it been billed as a support group for *men* rather than *fathers*, they would not have signed up. Joining for their children's sake was more acceptable than seeking help for their own grief and emotional well-being. To a man, the desire to help their children was the ticket in the door.

Joe, true to his no-nonsense manner, then said, "You know, I'll be honest. I almost didn't come tonight because, really, I am just *not* a 'support group kind of guy.'" Heads nodded around the table. That acknowledgment seemed to relieve some pressure in the room. None of the fathers had ever pictured himself as a "support group kind of guy." Of course, none had imagined being widowed at such a young age with children to raise, a home to manage, and lives to restore.

Not surprisingly, Bruce, as the most outgoing father, was the only one who had previously been to a support group. A couple of months earlier, he had gone to a meeting offered by the hospice organization that had cared for his wife. He walked into that session only to find that he was the youngest person there by a couple of decades. While certain aspects of grief are universal, Bruce's situation as a forty-four-year-old father with young children at home was fundamentally different from that of a seventy-six-year-old widow. The others were mourning spouses they had been married to for decades. He was grieving the loss of a future that had been taken away from him, while at the same time trying to figure out how to raise three grieving daughters by himself. Rather than finding connection and comfort, Bruce only felt different and more alone. He never went back to that group.

Both research findings and our own clinical observations leave little doubt that men are generally less open to seeking or accepting support than women. Societal expectations of male self-reliance and stoicism are not what they were generations ago, but these gender differences have endured. So, it is not surprising that women make up the overwhelming majority in bereavement groups. Even the phrase itself—"support group"—implies a degree of vulnerability or neediness that some men don't want to acknowledge in themselves. These biases provided a cultural backdrop against which the fathers decided to join our unique experiment.

The fathers began discussing what made their situations so challenging. They found common ground in precisely the circumstances that had isolated them elsewhere. They felt like third wheels around their married friends and couldn't quite relate to the parenting struggles of their divorced friends. The fathers in the group had not *chosen* to be single. Furthermore, being a widowed father didn't allow for weekends off or the episodic relief of shared parenting. Karl captured the difference by saying that he didn't think of himself as a "single" parent, but rather as an "only" or "sole" parent.

In the months since their wives' deaths, the fathers had received sympathy (and meals) from countless others. That support was invaluable. However, this night was the first chance any of them had to hear from and share with those who could truly understand what they were going through. Their connections with each other were immediate and frequent. ("I know exactly what you mean," several said.) The fathers were setting the tone for the group as a place to acknowledge self-doubt and insecurity, and to receive both understanding and practical advice.

The men talked for nearly two hours. Their exchanges were honest and direct. Sensing that their connections with each other would be more meaningful than the lectures we had planned, we asked if they would prefer meetings devoted entirely to group discussion. Their response was clear and we abandoned our plan to begin each session with a lecture.

Karl then questioned our decision to limit the intervention to six sessions, asking, "Why would we want to cut this short?" Several other fathers felt the same way and we decided to meet monthly on an open-ended basis. In other words, we changed the format, duration, and scope of the support group in response to what the men felt would best fit their needs. This was not going to be the educational or therapeutic intervention that we had initially envisioned. We had already begun to learn from these thoughtful and injured men.

After the fathers and their children went home, the two of us sat and reflected on the first meeting. We weren't entirely sure what we had started, but it struck us both that this work would be important to them and to us. We believed that the support group could help the fathers in their adjustment. Precisely how that would happen remained uncertain. We saw it as a positive sign that by the end of the meeting, the fathers had assumed some ownership of the group and how it would be conducted. And we learned a lesson that first night that would prove enduring: this group would work best as a collaboration between the fathers and us.

Our doubts about whether the initial meeting had been too difficult were put to rest the following month when everyone returned for the second meeting—including Dan. Still anxious and uncomfortable in a group setting, he at least felt less panicked this time. The evening opened with Neill bringing to the table the crisis with his daughter and how to mark the first anniversary of his wife's death.

The five men who would continue with the group were now in place and we would welcome two more fathers in the months ahead. They were already on their way toward building a partnership that would be instrumental in their healing. But this would take time. First, each man had to endure his own crash course in the complex and disorienting world of grief.

3

Beyond Death and Dying

I n the late 1960s, *LIFE* magazine was one of the most widely read and influential periodicals in the world. Renowned for its photojournalism, the general-interest magazine covered all aspects of American life. The November 21, 1969, edition was no exception. It included a review of what would be The Beatles' final studio album, a profile of Ohio State University head football coach Woody Hayes, and an advertisement for a commemorative book on that summer's moon landing. It also featured an article on a little-known University of Chicago psychiatrist, Dr. Elisabeth Kübler-Ross, and her groundbreaking work with terminally ill patients.

In an era when public discourse about death and dying was almost nonexistent and when many physicians believed that a patient was better off not knowing his or her prognosis, Kübler-Ross was encouraging candid and open conversations with people about their impending deaths. Her innovative approach and courage to challenge the status quo drew the

interest of *LIFE* editor Loudon Wainwright. His captivating story introducing Kübler-Ross and her new book, *On Death and Dying*, would forever change the national conversation about end-of-life and grief.

The article described Kübler-Ross's seminar teaching clinicians about
the experiences of terminally ill patients. Physicians, nurses, chaplains,
and medical students watched through a one-way mirror as she interviewed a twenty-two-year-old woman who had been diagnosed just two
weeks earlier with leukemia, which at that time was almost always fatal.
Large black-and-white pictures of the patient showed a vibrant and beautiful young woman with long hair and a wide smile. She looked nothing
like someone close to death, which in some ways was the point. She talked
about her diagnosis and understanding that leukemia would almost certainly kill her. Her willingness to openly discuss the prospect of her own
death must have been astounding to those observing the interview.

Kübler-Ross theorized that people facing their own mortality proceed
through five stages prior to their death. In the first stage, the person is
unable or unwilling to accept that he or she is going to die (Denial). After
reality sets in, the person experiences intense frustration (Anger). Next is
a period of negotiation, perhaps with God or the physician, in an effort
to delay the inevitable (Bargaining). In the fourth stage, sadness and
despair take hold when it becomes apparent that one's fate is unavoidable
(Depression). The fifth and final stage is characterized by reflection, perhaps enlightenment, and a readiness to "let go" (Acceptance). Kübler-Ross
offered a compelling roadmap for how people advance through each of
the five stages.

Thinking of grief as a predictable process resolved through linear and
well-defined steps has obvious appeal. In an era when discussion of death
and dying was considered taboo, Kübler-Ross's work offered a clear explanation of a complex and terrifying phenomenon. The five stages made
intuitive sense and were easy to understand.

The *LIFE* magazine article catapulted Kübler-Ross's version of the grief
process into the nation's consciousness. For nearly fifty years, her "five
stages of grief" has served as the predominant framework for how the
public understands grief resolution. Although Kübler-Ross's approach

was informed by her experiences with individuals anticipating their *own* deaths, many subsequently and widely understood it as applying to how we grieve after the death of *someone else.*

Just as professionals and laypeople alike extended her pilot work with dying patients to all death-related grief, they further invoked Kübler-Ross's stage theory to explain how people respond to just about any kind of loss: a failed relationship; a serious injury or medical condition; and even something as relatively trivial as fans' reactions to their favorite athlete retiring or being traded to another team. The "five stages of grief" is deeply ingrained in our cultural lexicon. Perhaps most importantly for the fathers in the support group, it was their default template for how they expected to feel after their wives died.

■

As an engineer, Karl had always relied on logic and his analytic skills to solve complex problems. His personality is well suited to this line of work. He approaches his job, and life in general, in a methodical and outcome-oriented fashion, striving to identify the problem and consider all possibilities before arriving at a solution. He excels in a world that is rooted in cause-and-effect relationships. The emotional world is a different matter altogether.

Karl had known for months that his wife was going to die, but he felt wholly unprepared for what followed. During Susan's illness, her medical needs dictated his priorities: taking her to doctor appointments; making sure she took the right medicines in the right dosages at the right times; and sitting up with her on those long nights after chemotherapy infusions. As miserable as that time had been, Karl was at least clear about his role: take care of his wife and help her battle cancer.

After Susan died, all sense of order and predictability was gone. Karl found the lack of clarity to be disorienting. He felt like he was in a fog. If asked what he fed his children for dinner the night before, he would not have remembered. He had trouble concentrating when he returned to work and he spent hours staring blankly at his computer screen, lost in thoughts of Susan and how everything had changed. Normally an efficient worker, Karl saw his productivity lag. He could manage well enough when assigned a specific task, but when asked to design and implement a new project, he uncharacteristically stalled. His existence felt completely foreign.

Karl had experienced loss before but nothing approaching the magnitude of Susan's death. His understanding of what was normal was shaped by a passing familiarity with the five stages of grief. To bring order to his world, Karl tried to match his emotional responses to one of the five stages. He figured that he was in the "anger" stage whenever he was the least bit irritable or short-fused with his children. When his sorrow lifted for brief periods of time and he had a good moment, Karl assumed that he was in "denial." He thought that he had reached the "depression" stage when his sadness felt crushing. But he was experiencing so much more. He felt guilty, regretful, and even relieved that Susan's suffering was over. It soon became apparent that there was nothing either linear or predictable about his grief. Although Karl was drawn to the clearly defined Kübler-Ross model, it neither matched nor fully accounted for all that he was going through.

■

Launching a support group for widowed fathers was a significant departure from our usual work at the cancer hospital. Our clinical responsibilities had been limited to the psychological and psychiatric care of patients undergoing active cancer treatment. Neither of us was an authority on bereavement at that time. Consequently, when we began meeting with the men, we were anxious to learn as much as we could about adaptation to catastrophic loss. The fathers deserved no less.

Our first step was to take a closer look at the basis for Kübler-Ross's stages of grief theory. Her detailed interviews with gravely ill patients undoubtedly yielded rich insight; however, her sample included just two hundred and fifty individuals. Importantly, the experience of anticipating your own death is different from grieving the death of another person. Initially, Kübler-Ross did not intend to describe how people grieve the deaths of others. Only after *On Death and Dying* gained such widespread popularity did she and others apply the "five stages of grief" more broadly. Further, very few carefully conducted research studies support the theory that grief progresses sequentially through stages. It became clear to us that the most well-known and frequently cited framework for understanding all grief reactions was based on a single observational series of individuals anticipating their own deaths. Viewed in this light, it is not surprising that Karl's experience did not fit neatly into the Kübler-Ross model.

The scope and quality of grief research has improved dramatically in recent decades. Subsequent studies, conducted with more methodological rigor, have demonstrated a very different set of normal grief trajectories that challenge the implied universality of Kübler-Ross's model. As a result, leaders in the field now appreciate that grief is a dynamic and highly variable process. Not surprisingly, no theories reliably predict the course or duration of grief that each person will experience. Ultimately, the absence of an agreed-upon, one-size-fits-all model may be the reason more recent research findings have not penetrated or shaped the public's imagination to nearly the same extent as Kübler-Ross's work did decades ago.

The terms *grief, mourning*, and *bereavement* refer to very closely related concepts. In general, grief is our response to the loss of someone (or something) with whom we had a connection. It includes how we feel (sadness, shock, guilt), how we act (crying, withdrawing from friends and family), how we think (indecision, confusion, rumination), and how our bodies respond (fatigue, poor sleep, change in appetite).

Mourning refers to the outward expression of grief in a way that reflects cultural, religious, and societal expectations. For example, funeral processions in New Orleans are famously accompanied by jazz music. In the Jewish tradition, the formal mourning period following the death of a parent continues for twelve months after the burial.

Whereas grief and mourning can follow the loss of anyone or anything considered meaningful, the term "bereavement" is used only in the context of death. The intensity and length of a person's bereavement depends on countless variables: the nature of the relationship with the person who died, prior experiences with loss, pre-existing psychological health, personality traits, circumstances surrounding the death, the level of available support, and concurrent stresses. Thus, it is no wonder that no two people are bereaved in precisely the same way.

Over the past few decades, scholars have introduced several new theories about how people cope with loss. In our view, the most compelling and practical framework for understanding the dynamic and individualized nature of grief is the Dual Process Model of Coping with Bereavement. Developed by Margaret Stroebe and Henk Schut, two psychologists at Utrecht University in the Netherlands, the Dual Process Model captures the essence of loss and adaptation in a simple and elegant fashion.

The Dual Process Model holds that how well a person adapts following the death of a loved one is determined by how well he or she copes with two distinct types of grief-related stressors. *Loss-oriented stressors* are those associated with the death itself and consist of thoughts and feelings that are most commonly associated with grief. These include dwelling on memories of the person who died, yearning for that person's companionship, ruminating on the circumstances surrounding the death, and longing for a future that will remain unfulfilled. *Restoration-oriented stressors* arise subsequent to, and as a direct result of, the death and relate to the challenges of restoring a life without the person who died. Examples include adapting to new housing and financial circumstances, negotiating changes in relationships, and adjusting to new or significantly altered roles and responsibilities.

A third and critical component of the Dual Process Model is *oscillation*, which refers to the process of shifting attention and effort between the loss- and restoration-oriented stressors. Since a person cannot feasibly contend with both types of stressors simultaneously, he or she must alternate—or oscillate—his or her focus between them. Ignoring either one prevents healthy adaptation. Failure to oscillate may lead to preoccupation with one type of stressor: either intense mourning without taking steps to move forward or a singular focus on the future without allowing time to work through the loss. The Dual Process Model also acknowledges that there are moments when pauses or "time-outs" from dealing with either type of stressor are both unavoidable and beneficial. Every once in a while, watching a mindless television show can be a perfect distraction.

The importance of oscillation is beautifully illustrated by a frustrating interaction Karl had with a friend soon after Susan's death. The friend approached Karl with a suggestion about how to approach mourning the death of his wife and managing the needs of his children. "Just think about what a flight attendant announces before every take off," his friend said. "'In case of an emergency, put on your *own* oxygen mask before attempting to help others with theirs.'" The inference was clear: Karl should focus on taking care of himself before trying to take care of his children. In the language of the Dual Process Model, Karl's friend was suggesting that he concentrate on his main loss-oriented stressor (his yearning for Susan) and delay attending to his most pressing restoration-oriented stressors (caring for his children).

Karl knew immediately that this advice was impractical, unhelpful, and impossible to follow. Putting on an oxygen mask takes a matter of seconds. How long would it take to "get over" Susan's death? Karl was not sure that would—or even should—ever happen. In reality, both loss- and restoration-oriented stressors were overwhelming him at the same time. The need to rapidly shift his attention from one to the other was inescapable.

■

In the weeks after Susan died, Karl thought of her constantly: while driving in his car, when sitting at his desk at work, while lying in bed at night. He remembered when they first met. He and Susan were alike in many ways. Both were scholarly, headstrong, and had high expectations of themselves and others. After ten years of a committed relationship, they got married but did not see the need to have children. Both were happy in their relationship and invested in their careers.

Things changed in 1996. Driving back to work one afternoon after dropping Susan off at the airport for a business trip, Karl was involved in a serious collision. Somehow, he escaped with only minor injuries but the other driver, who had fallen asleep at the wheel, was killed instantly. Deeply shaken, Karl emerged with a new perspective on life and vowed to prioritize relationships above all else. He and Susan decided to start a family. Within months, they were expecting their first child, a girl. Their second child, a son, was born three years later.

In the years following the accident, Karl made a point to attend as many family get-togethers as possible. One summer he, Susan, and the children—then seven and ten years old—were planning to fly to California to visit family. The morning before they were supposed to leave, Susan went to her doctor about a nagging cough that she had assumed was a Spring allergy. She expected to get a prescription and be on her way. Instead, the doctor ordered a chest X-ray as a precaution. He saw something suspicious and sent her directly to the hospital for further tests. There, MRI scans revealed that Susan—who had never smoked a single cigarette—had lung cancer. She and Karl canceled their travel plans and she saw an oncologist the following day. By the end of the week, additional scans showed that Susan's cancer had already spread to her bones and brain.

Treatment began immediately with radiation, followed by months of chemotherapy. By Thanksgiving, the tumors in her lungs were nearly undetectable. Susan and those close to her celebrated the news. Karl was relieved, but his enthusiasm was tempered. He had researched the survival rates for metastatic lung cancer and learned that even with initial treatment success, the long-term prognosis was grim. Although Karl made his living figuring out solutions to complex problems, this one was beyond his reach almost from the beginning. One day, he started to ask Susan whether she understood how serious her illness was. She stopped him before he could complete his thought and made it clear that she wasn't willing to discuss her mortality as Karl was suggesting. Her job was to focus on getting well. It was up to him to worry about everything else.

Months after the promising scan results, Susan's cancer returned, just as Karl had feared. She began an even more punishing chemotherapy regimen that ultimately gave her more time but came at a significant cost. She was exhausted nearly all of the time and the tumors in her brain increasingly affected the clarity of her thinking. The independent, driven woman who Karl had fallen in love with more than twenty years earlier was disappearing. Susan had planned to write letters for her children to open on their wedding days; she would not be there, but wanted them to have something from their mother. But with her mental state compromised, she never wrote those notes.

After Susan's death, Karl was left to navigate an unfamiliar world. He struggled to understand why his experiences didn't match what he thought he knew about grief. He, like all the fathers in the group, faced head-on the loss-oriented stressor aspect of the Dual Process Model. But each had restorative work to do too. They all had children to get to school, houses that needed cleaning, and jobs to keep.

4

Going It Alone

n the 2012 Olympics, the Jamaican national team set the world record in the men's 4 × 100 meter relay race with a time of 36.84 seconds. In the individual 400-meter event held four days earlier, Grenadian sprinter Kirani James clocked in at 43.94 seconds to win the gold medal. Each race covered the same distance and was run on the same track, yet the two winning times were separated by more than seven seconds. The reasons for the faster time are obvious. As part of a team, sprinters are already in full stride when handed the baton and can run at top speed for shorter distances without having to conserve energy. Tasks are accomplished more efficiently when more than one person can share the work. Still, success depends on smooth transitions. The best relay teams place as much emphasis on passing the baton as they do straight-line sprinting. Eventually, they develop a rhythm and seamless exchanges become second nature.

A similar dynamic had once existed between the fathers in our group and their wives when it came to raising their children. When they shared

and coordinated responsibilities, parenting was a more efficient and successful team effort. Over the course of their marriages, these couples
took on complementary roles in parenting their children and managing
their homes.

In one of the early meetings of the support group, Bruce described how
he and his wife, Lisa, had developed a well-established division of labor
throughout their fourteen years of marriage. Then it all went to hell. Lisa
had already endured radiation therapy, chemotherapy, numerous hospitalizations, and the surgical removal of part of her colon that left her in
pain and constantly fatigued. She had to lie in bed much of the day and
rarely had the strength or energy to enjoy time with her children. She was
desperate to feel better, and she and Bruce made an appointment for a
second opinion.

The consulting oncologist reviewed Lisa's medical history, the most
recent scans, and her long list of medications. He said that, unfortunately,
he had nothing different or better to suggest. Lisa and Bruce were disappointed, but they resigned themselves to continuing with the current treatment plan. They thanked the oncologist for his time and got up to leave.
Perhaps sensing that they did not fully appreciate Lisa's dire prognosis, the
oncologist asked them to sit back down. He paused briefly before speaking
directly to Lisa. "I feel it is important for you to understand that even with
treatment, you will likely only have weeks to live. Maybe months, at best.
I'm so sorry."

Lisa and Bruce were stunned. They had met with countless doctors
and specialists during the previous five months, yet this was the first time
anyone had said that she was going to die. Their goal—their expectation,
their plan—was for Lisa to survive her cancer. They had sought out the
second opinion with the hope of finding a less rigorous course of treatment. Instead, they were told their life together was quickly coming to
an end.

Lisa immediately began preparing her family for life without her. She
gave Bruce the usernames and passwords to their online accounts, showed
him how to arrange the children's summer schedules, and wrote letters

to each of their three daughters. She composed four "Family Rules" for the girls:

1. *Stay close and be each other's best friends.*
2. *Teach each other, especially about the girl stuff.*
3. *Team up on Dad when there's something special you want like a nice pair of shoes for the prom. You know how he can be tight with the wallet.*
4. *Support Dad when he is ready to date. He is going to need it.*

Lisa would have done more but she was exhausted and growing weaker by the day. Within two weeks of getting the second opinion, Lisa was admitted to the hospital where she fell into a coma and died.

After Bruce finished sharing his story with the group, one of us (Justin) asked whether the two weeks between the conversation with the oncologist and Lisa's death allowed for one last "passing of the baton." Bruce recoiled at the suggestion that this somehow could have been a smooth transition.

"*Passing* the baton? Are you kidding? More like it was *thrown* at me! In no way was I ready for—or even interested in taking—that baton, and I'm still trying to pick it up off the ground."

Bruce is an engaging man with a warm smile and quick wit. He greets everyone he meets with direct eye contact and a friendly pat on the shoulder. With a blend of sincerity and humor, he can win over a room in minutes. He has countless friends and acquaintances through his leadership positions at his church and the YMCA and can hardly go out for lunch without bumping into someone he knows. He is also prone to deep introspection and self-doubt, and he makes little effort to hide his insecurities. In fact, Bruce's authenticity and self-effacing humor are a big part of his charm.

After graduating from college, Bruce took a position at the YMCA, where he met Lisa, who was volunteering that summer as a camp counselor. He was quickly drawn to her spirited personality and got a kick out of how she never censored her opinions. Bruce spent the summer trying to convince Lisa to go out with him. For a brief period when they first dated, he was her supervisor. He would later joke that it was the last time he held the upper hand in their relationship.

After several years Bruce was ready to propose. He made reservations at an upscale restaurant with plans for an after-dinner stroll through downtown Raleigh to the steps of the Capitol building, where he would ask Lisa to marry him. He was nervous, but the evening had been going well. Toward the end of dinner, Lisa's demeanor changed. As they left the restaurant she complained, "It's too cold. Let's turn around, I want to go back inside." Bruce convinced her to go for the walk, but Lisa refused to hold his hand. Even though she was bundled up in her jacket, Lisa complained about the cold much of the way. "Geez, it isn't *that* cold," Bruce thought to himself. "What has gotten into her?"

As soon as they reached the Capitol steps Lisa said "Okay, great, we made it. Now, can we *please* go back?!?" She sounded uncharacteristically irritable. Fearing that the window for a romantic proposal was closing, Bruce hurriedly got down on one knee. Much to his relief, Lisa broke into a smile and said "yes."

It would be years before Lisa revealed that she had been toying with him the whole time. During dinner, when Bruce had gone to the bathroom, she had searched the pockets of his sport coat, suspecting this might be the night. She found a small, felt-covered box that was just the right size for an engagement ring and decided to have a little fun with her soon-to-be fiancé. Bruce could not help but be impressed. Not for the last time, Lisa had been one step ahead of him.

After they married, Bruce and Lisa had three daughters. The atmosphere at home was lively and filled with laughter. Being a playful and fun-loving dad came naturally to Bruce who was much more comfortable hugging his children than punishing them. Discipline, like many other necessary but less enjoyable jobs around the house, usually fell to Lisa. She was a dynamo who crammed twenty-five hours into a day and functioned as "the nerve center" of their family. She orchestrated the social calendar and involved herself in every aspect of her daughters' lives.

Eventually, Lisa got a job in her daughters' school, in part, just to stay in the loop.

With a family he adored and a rewarding career, Bruce had never been more content. At the end of the summer before the girls were set to enter first, fourth, and seventh grades, the family went on their annual vacation in West Virginia. Lisa's stomach had been bothering her for weeks and her pain only intensified while they were in the mountains. It never occurred to Bruce that her stomach discomfort might signal anything serious and he teased her about having to spend so much time in the bathroom. But Lisa's sister, a physician who was with them on vacation, was concerned and convinced Lisa to see a specialist when she got home.

The next week, Bruce was driving home from an out-of-town meeting when he called Lisa to see how her doctor's appointment had gone. She said that she would rather talk about it in person and asked him to come straight home. Bruce could tell she had been crying. He panicked. For the rest of the drive, he imagined the worst while trying to convince himself that he was overreacting. When he walked in the front door, Lisa was sitting on the couch with box of tissues in her lap, holding her mother's hand. The colonoscopy had revealed a tumor so large that the doctors had to use a pediatric scope to maneuver around it.

After nearly five months of treatment, the once-massive tumor had shrunk to a size that the surgeons could remove it. But the hope that the operation would be a turning point faded as Lisa's health deteriorated. Follow-up scans showed multiple new tumors. It seemed to Bruce as if taking out the original tumor had somehow caused the cancer to spill throughout his wife's body.

Hours after Lisa died, Bruce drove home in the dark. He greeted the family friend who had been watching his daughters and walked upstairs to their bedrooms. He carried his two youngest girls into their older sister's room, where he told them together that Mom had died.

All at once, Bruce was the only runner in what had been a two-parent relay team. He remembered a time several years earlier when Lisa had gone out of town for the weekend with some friends. For three full days, Bruce took care of the children by himself. He cooked meals, drove carpools, settled squabbles, arranged playdates, gave baths, and maintained bedtime routines. He kept it fun but was utterly exhausted by the time Lisa returned home. Bruce greeted her at the door with a kiss and said, "Welcome home, Hon. The kids are yours, I'm going to lie down."

Now, Bruce was solely responsible for his children's well-being and knew that he would be unable to parent as adeptly as when Lisa was alive. In the midst of his deep grief over the loss of the only woman he had ever loved, he was struck by all the ways he was no match for Lisa's parenting competence.

An internment ceremony for family and close friends was held a couple of months after Lisa died, on what would have been her fortieth birthday. Bruce's daughters were tearful but mostly held their composure, as they had for much of the previous two months. After they returned home that afternoon, his oldest daughter, Olivia, ran straight upstairs. Bruce assumed that she needed some time by herself. A short while later, Bruce's mother, who was in town for the service, sat down beside him on the living room couch. She began by saying, "Don't worry, everything is fine, but Olivia had her first period this afternoon. She was upset at first but she is now resting in her room."

Bruce's heart sank. How unfair for Olivia that it had happened on this particular day. He then realized he had never talked with her about what to do or expect for her first period—not that he even knew what to say. This was a conversation that she was supposed to have had with her mother, but Bruce wasn't sure if that talk had ever taken place. Their lives had been consumed by Lisa's cancer treatment and so much had slipped through the cracks. Had talking with Olivia about her first period been one of those things?

Bruce gathered himself and walked upstairs. He sat on the foot of his daughter's bed, where she was lying with her eyes closed. "Grandma told me what happened. Are you okay?"

Olivia nodded silently, keeping her eyes shut. Bruce could hardly blame her for not wanting to talk. After all, he had no words of wisdom, no stories of his own experience. None of the things that Lisa could have offered. He wondered what his daughter was thinking but didn't know how to ask.

Instead, he said that he loved her and would be downstairs if she wanted to talk. She nodded again.

That night, while lying in bed, Bruce revisited the events of the day. Lisa was gone and the day had reinforced how unprepared he felt for what lay ahead. With two daughters yet to hit puberty, this was just the beginning. There was so much to learn and so many things he had no clue about: menstrual cycles, shopping for training bras, fashion, dating, "the talks" about sex. Bruce never thought he would have to carry the baton alone.

5

The Wrong Parent Died

"Absolutely. One-hundred percent," Neill answered without hesitation.

Karl repeated his question. "Do you *really* believe your children would be better off if you had died instead of your wife?"

"It's not even close," Neill said. He quickly counted off all the things Deanna had done for their family, detailing her involvement in just about every aspect of their children's lives. She was simply a much more important cog in the family wheel. "You guys helped me out with my daughter and the hockey game situation, but Deanna would have handled it on her own." Neill concluded, "So, yes, for my children's sake, there's no question that the wrong parent died."

The discussion leading up to the exchange between Neill and Karl had coalesced around the familiar topic of parental competence—or, as the men often saw it, parental *in*competence. Karl had shared his latest blunder, which occurred when he took his two children on a family trip to Connecticut for a wedding. As they were leaving their hotel room for the ceremony, Karl noticed for the first time how his children were dressed.

"So, there's my ten-year-old son wearing this pair of khakis that don't come close to fitting him. The pant legs stopped about three inches above his ankles and he couldn't even button the pants because the waistband was so tight. He looked ridiculous, but they were the only pair of pants I'd brought for him to wear." Yet another instance of being unprepared, something Karl hated. "I'm standing there looking at my son in the hallway of this hotel and I think to myself, 'No way this happens if Susan were still here.'"

"I know just what you mean," Neill said. "Deanna did so many things better than I'm doing them now. I feel like I'm screwing up pretty much all the time." Then he said the words that caught Karl by surprise: "The wrong parent died."

Neill had never been comfortable opening up about his feelings. He joined the support group only for his children's sake. If they were going to be stuck with the "wrong parent," he figured that he owed it to them to be the best wrong parent he could be. He thought that being with other single, bereaved fathers might help him, even though his wife had died from a sudden respiratory infection, not cancer.

Neill was working for a private healthcare company when he first met his future wife. He was tasked with negotiating reimbursement rates with the state and was paired up with a representative from the social services department. That person was Deanna. The negotiation was challenging, required numerous meetings, and dragged on for months. This turned out to be a blessing, as their working relationship evolved into something more. Once their work together was complete, Neill and Deanna immediately began dating. They married within the year and would raise two sons and two daughters.

As Neill advanced in his career, his work and travel demands increased. Along the way, the bulk of parenting and household responsibilities fell to Deanna who also worked a part-time job. She handled nearly everything at home: meal planning, homework, carpools, pediatrician appointments, class field trips, birthday parties, and countless other things that were lost on Neill at the time. Deanna managed all these responsibilities despite a series of persistent headaches, achy joints, and chronic fatigue that began soon after their fourth child was born. After years without an explanation for her symptoms, she was diagnosed with lupus. With treatment, she finally found some relief.

One November, Deanna started to feel extremely weak and developed a fever. A chest X-ray revealed pneumonia. She was prescribed antibiotics and told to rest. At the time, being sick was more of an inconvenience than a serious worry. With a household to run, four children to manage, and the holidays approaching, lying in bed seemed like a waste of valuable time.

Deanna's high fever persisted and she was admitted to the hospital several days later. Even then, Neill was not especially alarmed. For years, he had seen his wife cope with her chronic illness with such composure and determination that he expected her to manage this episode the same way. It wasn't until Deanna's oxygen levels dropped precipitously and she was transferred to the intensive care unit that Neill became frightened. She was nearing the point where she would need mechanical ventilation, meaning she would have to be heavily sedated until she could breathe on her own again. The doctors gave Neill and Deanna a few minutes alone before taking her to anesthesia. Leaning over the hospital bed, Neill smiled to hide his fear. He stroked the back of his wife's hand, tried to assure her that she would be fine, and promised to be there when she woke up.

For the next several days, Neill stayed by Deanna's side, nervously watching the monitors and asking the doctors for assurances that they couldn't give. When they described how Deanna was not responding to the new round of antibiotics, he could sense the pessimism in their voices. Late one evening, her pulse weakened and her blood pressure plummeted. Deanna died shortly before midnight, one week before Thanksgiving.

Neill's life had changed in an instant. He returned home the next morning as a widowed man and his children's only parent. The suddenness of Deanna's illness and the speed with which her health deteriorated had not allowed for any kind of parenting transition. Neill was convinced that no amount of preparation would have made a difference.

"I get why you think the wrong parent died. I do," Karl said, responding to Neill's unyielding stance. He too had wondered whether his children's lives would have been better if their mother had been the surviving parent. Ultimately, this kind of thinking struck him as self-pity and he dismissed it as unproductive. Besides, Karl said, it was not as if he—or any of the guys seated around the table that night—were mindless idiots incapable of raising their children.

"When I noticed how my son was dressed, I managed to find the nearest department store and bought him a pair of pants that fit," Karl pointed out. The whole episode had been embarrassing, but he had handled it.

"You just can't allow yourself to think like that, Neill. That's not being fair to yourself. In an ideal world, your children would have *both* parents. It's not your fault that they don't have that."

Neill was unmoved. "I hear you, but I'm just looking at it realistically. And, realistically, my children would be better off with their mother instead of me. It's just that simple. Maybe one day I'll see it your way, but I doubt it. Besides, if you ask me, there's just something worse about losing your mom."

Disagreements like this exchange between Neill and Karl reflected how far the group had come in just several months. The men were now comfortable enough with each other to share opposing views. As widowed fathers, they had much in common, but owning similar histories and facing comparable challenges did not mean that they were responding in exactly the same fashion. The men were in the same boat, but they were not the same people. Their growing trust prompted honest and, at times, spirited exchanges about what mattered most to them. It was an important moment in the group's maturation.

The brief debate between Karl and Neill also produced an unintended but welcome result. By trying to convince Neill of his importance as a father, Karl found himself defending his own parental relevance. Initially, he had relayed the story from his trip to Connecticut to illustrate his inability to keep up with the cascade of family details. He had even explicitly noted that his wife would have handled that situation better than he had. But, in the end, Karl had managed just fine. By encouraging Neill to be more charitable with himself, Karl demonstrated a successful resolution of a restoration-oriented stressor.

Despite the seriousness of the topics discussed in group meetings, the tone was not always negative or somber. Increasingly, humor found its way into their conversations and usually highlighted the absurdity of their plights as sole fathers. The jokes were often self-deprecating and, at times, had a dark edge.

"Well, I don't know whether or not my children lost the *wrong* parent," Bruce piped in, "but I'm a strong contender for the 'Worst Father of the Year' award." He described a dinner at home with his girls (the rare evening when he wasn't shuttling them to play rehearsal, dance practice, or piano lessons) when he noticed that his middle daughter, Marcy, was wearing new shoes. He asked where she got them.

"Mrs. Sanders bought them for me," she said almost under her breath, continuing to look down.

"Wait, what? Mrs. Sanders from *school*? Why would your teacher buy you new shoes?"

Marcy reluctantly told her father how the stitching on her old pair had become so frayed that one of the soles had become partially detached. While walking back to class from recess, her teacher noticed the shoe flapping in the hallway. Sympathetic to what Marcy had been through since losing her mother, Mrs. Sanders used her lunch break to go shopping.

"I'm sorry, Dad. I did ask you, like, three times. But it's okay, really, I know you've been busy."

Bruce felt horrible. His child was walking around with a pair of broken-down shoes and he had not even noticed. He wondered how many other things he was missing. Worse, his daughter had hesitated to tell him what her teacher had done out of fear that it would make him feel guilty. She was protecting him.

With the other guys in the support group, Bruce was able to joke about his shortcomings without fear of criticism. "So Karl, while you may have dressed that poor son of yours in high waters, at least you actually provided him clothing! I mean, seriously, having a teacher buy shoes for your kid? I can promise you that Lisa never would have sent our child to school dressed like that. She's probably looking down at me right now, shaking her head."

Neill seemed particularly interested—perhaps reassured—to hear of Bruce's parenting failures. "Have you heard back from the teacher?" he asked.

"Can you even imagine what the teachers at that school must think about me?" Bruce said, laughing. "'Poor guy, in way over his head, can't even keep up with his child's basic needs.'"

"So now you're a charity case," Karl teased.

Increasingly, joking with one another about material too risky to share with outsiders was an important ingredient in the fathers' mutual healing. Had Bruce shared the story of his daughter's shoe incident with friends or family, he may have gotten advice in return. Or worse yet, pity. But in a room full of guys intimately familiar with the feeling of failure, guys who may also have children sporting worn-out shoes, it was cathartic and bonding.

Bruce kept the conversation moving. "Joe, what's up with you these days? Any big screw-ups?"

"Lots," Joe said with a slight grin. "You ought to see my laundry room. It's one big pile of wrinkled up, unfolded clothes. I pretty much just take them straight out the dryer and throw them on top of the pile. My kids search through and pick out clothes to get dressed. Seriously, it's a freaking mess in there.

"I'll tell you something, though. I have looked at that pile every day for a month straight. I know how to fold clothes and I know I need to do something about it. I'm not sure if it's normal to feel this way or not, but, honestly, right now . . . I just don't give a shit."

6

"Of Course I'm Depressed, but Do I Have Depression?"

W hat's the difference between being very shy and having social phobia? Or between a "neat freak" and a person who suffers from obsessive-compulsive disorder? Or a particularly fidgety schoolboy and a child with attention-deficit hyperactivity disorder? Distinctions between the outer bounds of "normal" and "pathological" are ubiquitous in modern life and not easy to make. People who experience loss respond in different ways, with varying degrees of intensity, and for different lengths of time. Mental health professionals find these responses difficult to predict. For example, leaders in the bereavement field have disagreed sharply and for a long time about how to define normal and abnormal grief.

This professional disagreement about grief and bereavement made headlines when the American Psychiatric Association (APA) considered changing its *Diagnostic and Statistical Manual of Mental Disorders (DSM)*.

Every fifteen to twenty years, the APA revises the *DSM*—which establishes the criteria clinicians use to diagnose psychiatric disorders—to incorporate the latest scientific research and contemporary expert opinion. Before the most recent edition (*DSM-5*) came out, the APA considered two grief-related proposals that sparked very heated debate.

The most controversial proposal suggested modifying how professionals diagnose major depression. The previous edition of the *DSM* specified that clinicians could not consider someone to have major depression if that person had lost a loved one less than two months earlier. The APA intended this "bereavement exclusion" to keep mental health professionals from mistaking grief for clinical depression. Clinical researchers Sidney Zisook, MD, at the University of California at San Diego and Katherine Shear, MD, at the Columbia University School of Social Work led one side of the debate. They argued that professionals should diagnose clinical depression even in the context of bereavement as they would following any other stressful life event such as divorce or the loss of a job. Zisook and Shear thought that people could experience both grief and depression simultaneously. Perhaps most importantly, they said, people who had clinical depression during early bereavement were no less deserving of treatment for their depression.

Many mental health professionals voiced opposition, none more vigorously than Jerome Wakefield, PhD, a clinical researcher at New York University. His position was that grief experienced immediately after a death is fundamentally different from depression unrelated to bereavement. He worried that eliminating the "bereavement exclusion" from the *DSM* would lead clinicians to diagnose depression in people who were not actually depressed. If a person reports that he or she had experienced low mood, poor concentration, fatigue, decreased appetite, or insomnia for two weeks, that person—according to the diagnostic criteria—had major depression. Yet those symptoms are also typical of grief. Wakefield noted that changing these criteria would mean that a person could be diagnosed with major depression just two weeks after losing a loved one.

The APA had another controversial decision to make: whether to create a new diagnosis for prolonged and debilitating grief. Two research groups submitted their suggestions, both with slightly different names and criteria. Drs. Shear, Zisook, and colleagues suggested "complicated grief," and Holly Prigerson, PhD, then at Harvard Medical School and the Dana-Farber Cancer Institute, and her colleagues advocated for "prolonged grief disorder." Both groups argued that unresolved and dysfunctional grief constitutes a distinct psychiatric condition. And both groups cited research that people who suffered more intensely or for an unusually long period of time warranted specific treatment.

Again, Dr. Wakefield led the opposition. He objected to the idea that grief should be classified as a mental illness. Like other leaders in the field, he feared that "pathologizing" grief as a psychiatric condition would stigmatize a common and normal human reaction. Dr. Wakefield also questioned whether the alternative proposals had sufficiently distinguished "complicated" from "uncomplicated" grief.

Following years of deliberation, the APA published the *DSM-5* in 2013 without the bereavement exclusion for major depression. This change means that clinicians use their judgment to distinguish between uncomplicated grief and major depression during early bereavement. In our opinion, this was a wise decision. Mental health professionals make similar clinical determinations every day. However, the APA task force did not identify in the *DSM-5* a disorder called either "complicated grief" or "prolonged grief disorder." Instead, it created what we consider an inelegant amalgam, "persistent complex bereavement-related disorder." The APA concluded that this condition requires further study.

Given the ongoing controversy about what constitutes normal grief, it is little wonder that when facing a mountain of unfolded laundry, Joe wondered whether it was normal for him to not give a shit.

■

Joe and Joy started dating during their senior year of college. At the time, Joe was more interested in the social scene than his classwork. Not Joy. She took her studies seriously and approached them with the same tirelessness that would come to define her legal career. She carried herself with an air of self-assuredness that came from her commitment to work harder than those around her.

As an assistant district attorney, Joy passionately advocated for society's less privileged, particularly women who were victims of domestic abuse and sexual assault. She hated that these cases were often settled with a plea bargain because the judicial system was overburdened or because many of these women lacked the resources to fight in court. Joy leveraged her position as the president of the county's bar association to enact change. She created a special division that was dedicated to aggressively prosecuting these cases, which would serve as a model for other district attorney offices around the state.

Joe and Joy balanced their careers with a full home life. They had two daughters in middle school and a son in preschool when Joy became pregnant with their fourth child. Since she was forty years old at the time, Joy underwent an amniocentesis to test for birth defects or chromosomal abnormalities. The results indicated that their baby had Down syndrome. Joy was determined from that moment on to fight for her child, a daughter they would name Grace, with the same tenacity she had put to use for her disadvantaged clients in the courtroom.

Grace was still in diapers when one morning Joy felt a lump in her breast. Within the week, she was diagnosed with breast cancer. She took a leave of absence from work and immediately started treatment. Since Joe worked from home, he was able to be with Joy at each phase of her therapy. He drove her to daily radiation appointments, sat with her during daylong chemotherapy infusion sessions, and helped her recover from two surgeries. Joy's treatment was punishing. It was also effective, and with her cancer in remission, life slowly returned to normal.

While at home one evening, about a year after being declared cancer-free, Joy lost her balance and fell. Days later, she fell again. The cancer had returned and was now affecting her brain. She enrolled in an experimental trial that required her to travel to Boston several times a month while Joe stayed at home with the children. Despite the aggressive approach, the tumors continued to spread. Exhausted and dispirited, Joy readied herself for each successive treatment. In time, her oncologist recommended hospice.

For the last month of her life, Joy mostly stayed in the hospital bed set up in their living room. Uncharacteristically subdued, she saved her energy for her children, including Grace who was now in Kindergarten. Several days before she died, she looked at Joe and asked whether he believed— really, actually believed—that she was going to die. She, of course, knew the answer, but it still felt unreal. Joe laid his head down beside her and quietly stroked her arm.

During the weeks and months after the funeral, Joe struggled to carry on. Just getting out of bed felt like a chore. He drifted through his morning routine, but Grace needed a lot of help. Joy had always insisted that her youngest daughter look as put-together as possible. She knew that having Down syndrome put Grace at risk for being teased and resolved that her appearance would not invite added pity or ridicule. Joe felt the weight of Joy's expectations each morning as he made sure Grace's outfit matched, brushed her long brown hair, and tightly fastened her hair bow so it wouldn't fall out.

Once the children were off to school, Joe was left alone with his thoughts and an empty house. Being able to work from home had always been one of the best parts of his job. During Joy's illness, the flexibility to set his own schedule allowed him to be there for much of her treatment. But the freedom that had once been a blessing now felt like a curse. The house felt lonely and uncomfortably quiet. Reminders of Joy were everywhere. Pictures of their family hung on the living room walls. Plaques and awards from her years at the district attorney's office filled the study. Joy's medications and pill bottles still cluttered the bathroom countertop, and her side of the bed remained undisturbed.

For the first time in his life, Joe felt disinterested in his future. He didn't eat much, and even though he was exhausted, he couldn't sleep. Everything seemed to take more effort. In time, his self-confidence eroded. When he tried to re-focus on his job, his normal motivation and drive were gone. The career that Joe had devoted years to building no longer seemed important. Whether he made a sale or got positive feedback from his boss made little difference to him.

Joe questioned whether he had been *too* focused on work all these years. Perhaps, he wondered, it took losing his wife to realize that family was what *really* mattered. But when being honest with himself, Joe knew that playing the "perspective card" was mostly an excuse. The reason he was floundering at work was the same reason why he sat alone at home instead of meeting friends for lunch. It was why, despite the parade of prepared meals delivered by his neighbors, he struggled to put dinner on the table and why he never bothered to fold the piles of laundry. Sad, lonely, and overwhelmed, he was depressed.

Of course, Joe was not the only father in the group to feel this way. Some were managing better than others, but all were familiar with feeling depressed. Their experiences closely mirrored the findings from the research we had been conducting with a larger group of their peers. Over four hundred fathers whose wives had died from cancer and who were raising children at home completed a detailed survey in our study of the psychological functioning and parenting challenges of widowed fathers.

Nearly all the men reported being solely responsible for their children's care. As expected, they reported high levels of stress about meeting the demands of being the only parent. Most striking, however, was the magnitude of their grief and depressive symptoms. Nearly two-thirds experienced clinically significant depressive symptoms within the first six months after their wives' deaths. Remarkably, roughly half of these men had high levels of depression two years later. Our findings suggest that widowed fathers are at heightened risk for intense and prolonged symptoms of grief.

In considering what constitutes normal and abnormal bereavement, the *DSM-5* specifies that an adult exhibiting sufficient grief symptoms twelve months following a death meets criteria for "persistent complex bereavement-related disorder." Our findings raise questions about the typical or normal duration of bereavement among widowed fathers—and by extension among other groups as well.

The men who responded to our survey closely echoed themes that had emerged in support group discussions. Those we surveyed expressed shock ("I seem to have lost the ability to judge the passage of time. It feels as if time is standing still"); sadness ("I spend each day fighting a sadness that won't go away"); isolation ("I have a very powerful feeling of being trapped, and being trapped makes me lonely"); rumination ("I'm left with memories of my wife in a very diminished, suffering, miserable state. I can't stop thinking about her last hours on Earth"); and despair ("It feels unbearable at times").

The emotional toll of losing their spouses was compounded by relentless fatigue ("My time and energy are all taken up with work, my daughter, and basic life maintenance. It seems endless"); carrying the parenting burden alone ("this will be my first summer as a single parent; I have no idea how to handle the kids while trying to work—and haven't had time to plan"); and filling the roles of both parents ("I am a good Dad, but I don't think I'm a great mother"; "I don't have that mothering instinct").

Revisiting the Dual Process Model helps us understand these grief reactions and the elements that contribute to intense and prolonged bereavement. Joe's daily struggles provide an apt example of loss-oriented stressors, restoration-oriented stressors, and the oscillation between them. Although he wanted to sleep in, each morning demanded that Joe get the kids up, dressed, fed, and off to school. Upon returning to his empty house, he could think of little else besides Joy's absence and the future they would never share. Often, Joe felt like he spent his days flipping between channels: kids; Joy; work; Joy; laundry; Joy. He was exhausted and desperately wanted a break from his grief and his two full-time jobs.

On most days, Joe and the other fathers in the group muddled through on their own. As a rule, they were reluctant to seek help or share their struggles with friends and family, with the exception of the monthly meetings where they could let their guard down, share stories, and crowdsource parenting advice. Some were clearly depressed, and perhaps a few met the criteria for "persistent complex bereavement-related disorder." However, on the third Monday of every month, they felt engaged, connected, and increasingly hopeful.

7

Band of Brothers

The group dynamic had changed over the first six months. The fathers' initial apprehension had been replaced by a shared understanding of their work together. During the first several meetings, we had been more active in leading the discussion. Increasingly, the men took ownership of each session. They set the agenda and wasted little time getting down to business. Perhaps most importantly, they felt part of something special and clearly began to care about each other. We noticed that when the fathers arrived for group meetings, they were more likely to give each other a hug than the formal handshakes that had marked the early months. Similarly, the men would often remain talking with each other in the parking lot well after the sessions ended.

Prior to the seventh meeting, two fathers who had recently lost their wives and had heard about our program contacted us about joining the group. We asked the five current members whether they were open to including new fathers. Not surprisingly, they were unanimous and enthusiastic about the idea. The following month, Russ and Steve attended their first meeting.

Russ is a former Marine and a man of few words. When he does speak, he is direct and straight to the point. After introducing himself, Russ described the day less than a year earlier when his own nightmare began. He was in New York City for business when a neighbor called to tell him that his wife, Kelley, had been taken to the hospital with sudden abdominal pain. Russ caught the first flight out of LaGuardia and was waiting for her by the time she got out of emergency surgery to remove her gall bladder.

Over the next several days, Kelley recovered and the worst seemed to be behind her. Then the pathology report came back positive for gall bladder cancer. Her doctor mentioned the possibility of a lab error, since this diagnosis is so rare in women Kelley's age. He wanted to re-run the tests and meet the following week to discuss the results. In the meantime, Russ and Kelley tried to learn as much as they could. They were terrified by what they discovered. When Kelley's doctor confirmed the initial pathology report, they knew that her chances of survival were remote. Russ sat stoically, holding his wife as the oncologist told her how long she had to live: with treatment, six months.

Russ and Kelley had been together for fifteen years. She had an easy laugh and everyone she met liked her immediately. Her warm demeanor revealed nothing of the poverty and instability she experienced as a child raised by a single mother in the rough neighborhoods of Camden, New Jersey. Russ marveled that such a happy and content person could emerge from such a troubled background.

Early in her marriage to Russ, Kelley had reason to call on the resiliency she had fostered as a child. The couple's firstborn son, whom they named Jordan, was born with a major heart defect. As a temporary fix, he underwent open heart surgery but would need a transplant to survive. After several agonizing months, a donor heart became available. Russ and Kelley alternated sleeping on the fold-out couch in the pediatric intensive care unit as their son recovered from the second major surgery of his young life. Tragically, Jordan's body rejected the donor heart, and he died. Russ and Kelley were devastated. They mourned their son and the dream of building a family together. In time, they began to move forward. Russ leaned on Kelley, who led the way with a relentlessly positive outlook and a resolve not to allow tragedy to define their lives. Two years later, they welcomed another son. Five years after that, a second healthy boy.

Kelley's capacity to adapt would once again be tested as she began her cancer treatment—now complicated by a painful abdominal hernia. She was given two choices: surgically repair the hernia, which would delay the start of her cancer treatment; or begin chemotherapy immediately and endure a higher level of pain. More than anything else, Kelley longed to see her sons grow up. She started chemotherapy without delay. Her pain, nausea, and vomiting were unrelenting and she rarely left her bed other than for appointments at the hospital. Her boys, now thirteen and eight years old, were frightened by it all. Unsure how to act around their mother, they stayed away from her bedroom.

After several months of chemotherapy failed to shrink her tumors, Kelley started to prepare Russ for life without her. Her instructions were clear:

> *Don't let the boys fall in with the wrong crowd.*
> *Check in with their school counselors twice a year.*
> *Listen patiently when one of them has a rough day at school.*
> *Make sure they get good grades.*
> *Make sure they go to college.*

Russ hated these conversations, but Kelley was persistent and had instructions for him as well:

> *Remarry and find happiness again.*

When Russ rejected her suggestion, Kelley insisted: "If not for yourself, then do it for our boys."

Kelley spent the last month of her life in a hospice facility so that her pain could be better managed. Russ stayed with her during the daytime and returned home in the evenings to be with their children. Before he left each day, Kelley reviewed her instructions to make sure he "got it." She was passing the baton for the final time.

Once she was gone, Russ came to appreciate and rely on Kelley's daily instructions. However, there was one directive that was particularly difficult for him to follow: "After I die, be sure to talk about me around the boys. Make sure they remember their Mom." Russ struggled to integrate Kelley's memory into discussions with his sons, fearing that the mere mention of their mother would only upset them. He knew that it would be difficult to talk about Kelley without becoming emotional himself and he didn't want the boys to see him as being weak. Soon, a conspiracy of silence took root: Russ rarely brought up Kelley's name and the boys followed his lead.

Joe immediately connected with Russ's struggle to help his sons grieve. "That's been really hard for me, too. My son is around the same age as yours. I've had a tougher time talking with him than with my daughters. That may be because my two girls are so much older, it's just easier to have conversations with them. And then with Grace, she actually brings up her mother all the time, so that's easier. But it's been different with my son. Maybe it's a 'guy thing.'"

Joe described how his son had recently been sent to the principal's office for acting up in class and subsequently melted down. "From what the teacher said, it was like the dam sprung a leak. She said he could barely talk and was sobbing uncontrollably."

Since that day, communication between Joe and his son had been better. "I now make a point of checking in with him. Especially if he seems off or upset while doing something minor, like chores, I'll stop and put my arm around him and ask how he's doing. Usually he says he's fine, but a couple of times he's talked about missing his Mom."

Russ and his sons weren't having those kinds of conversations. Instead, they had turned one of the end tables in the den into something of a shrine to Kelley. The boys had arranged pictures of the four of them together, photos of their mother from when she was younger, various mementos such as necklaces and earrings, and five block letters that spelled out M-O-M-M-Y. "I don't know if it is weird or not to have something like that sitting up in our house for everyone else to see," Russ said.

Dan, who typically remained quiet during group meetings, on this night made a point of identifying with Russ's reserved nature and his difficulty talking with his children about their mother. Perhaps as a "veteran" of the group, he sensed that he had something valuable to offer. "My best advice to you, Russ, is to *not* touch that shrine without talking to your kids about it first."

Dan's wisdom was hard earned. Several months earlier, he had made what he thought was a minor change to his living room furniture. One of the chairs was faded and tattered around the edges, so Dan bought a slipcover to fit over it. When his children got home from school that afternoon, his daughter looked at the chair and screamed, "What happened!?!" Dan's son immediately ripped off the new cover, ran to the garage, and stuffed it in the trash can.

Before Dan could ask why they were so upset, his daughter yelled, "How could you do that to Mom's chair?!" It had been where Sarah used to sit when the family watched TV or a home movie together. Where she wrote her lesson plans for Sunday School. More recently, where she rested while recovering from chemotherapy. To Dan's children, that chair symbolized their mother. And he had covered it up.

"I had been thinking that my kids were doing okay," Dan shared with Russ and the rest of the guys. "But now I'm not so sure. They still don't want to talk about her much. It's just hard to tell what's going on in their heads."

"I appreciate you guys telling me that. It's actually good to hear that it's not just me," Russ said. "I guess it's all right to talk about that kind of stuff in here, right?"

With impeccable timing, Bruce deadpanned, "Are you kidding, man? We take comfort in each other's misery all the time!"

■

All the men in the group were familiar with feelings of regret and guilt. Like the others, Steve often replayed in his mind the images of his wife's final hours. Most poignantly, he worried that he had failed her in her last moments.

He introduced himself to the group as the father of three children, all under the age of seven. His wife, Catie, had been diagnosed with cancer while pregnant with their third child. The first sign was a throbbing pain in her right shoulder. Catie's doctor initially diagnosed arthritis and reassured her that it was not a serious concern. That changed one morning when she woke up with piercing pain and a swollen right arm. This time, the doctors ordered scans which revealed a large tumor in her shoulder and smaller ones surrounding her left eye. The diagnosis was Ewing's sarcoma, an aggressive type of bone cancer that is rare in adult women.

Catie's pregnancy complicated her treatment. Under normal circumstances, she would have had surgery and started radiation therapy immediately. Instead, both of these treatments would be delayed until after she gave birth. Catie began a reduced chemotherapy regimen with hopes that she would carry the baby to at least thirty-six weeks. However, at thirty weeks, her amniotic fluid levels dropped and a fetal monitor suggested that the baby was in distress. Catie underwent an emergency C-section and gave birth to a daughter weighing just over two pounds.

Days later, surgeons removed the large tumor as well as parts of Catie's collar bone and shoulder. The next week, she started daily radiation therapy followed by the resumption of chemotherapy, this time at a higher dose. As Catie's treatment intensified, Steve's focus was divided between her, their newborn daughter, and their two older children, who were missing Mom and Dad. During Catie's hospitalization, Steve shuttled between home, the neonatal intensive care unit, and the adult cancer floor. Unable to be with her baby, Catie had Steve bring daily pictures and medical updates until she went home several weeks later.

After nine months of chemotherapy, Catie was in remission and had fewer hospital appointments to attend. The baby showed no obvious ill effects from being born prematurely or having been exposed to her mother's chemotherapy, and the two oldest children responded well to the return of a familiar rhythm. Steve was back at work and Catie's mother, who had moved in to help out, returned home to Tennessee. As arduous as the past year had been, Steve and Catie felt that they had escaped catastrophe. The worst, it seemed, was behind them.

Later that year, shortly before Christmas, Catie began having problems breathing. Scans confirmed their fears: the cancer was back and had now spread to her lungs. She immediately enrolled in a clinical trial, but the tumors continued to grow. When her doctors suggested hospice, Catie resisted. She told them that she was willing to try something—anything—to extend her life, desperate to survive as long as possible for her three young children. The oncologist agreed to try an experimental chemotherapy, but this too failed.

With no treatment options left, Steve and Catie sat down with their two older children—now four and six years old—and told them that their mother was not going to get better. Their oldest child, a thoughtful and sensitive boy who had always impressed his parents as being an "old soul," seemed to understand. But he wasn't ready to stop trying. "Call doctors in other states and other countries—like Russia—to see if they have anything. Or call the veterinarian. Maybe there's an animal medicine that people doctors haven't thought of yet."

Catie died at home, very early one morning before the sun had risen. Steve waited for the children to wake up. He tried to assure them that everything was going to be all right, even though he didn't believe it himself. After several minutes, his middle daughter said she was hungry. Exhausted, in shock, and without direction, Steve decided to take them out for donuts. He strapped the children, still in their pajamas, into their car seats and steered the minivan to the nearest breakfast spot. There, he sat in dazed silence as his children ate their breakfasts. Steve would later think to himself that it was such an odd thing to do at that moment—to go out for donuts just hours after his wife had died. But his children were hungry and needed to be fed. That responsibility, like so many others, now fell solely on him.

In the following months, Steve coped better than he had expected. He was so busy that he barely had time to grieve. The mornings were a blur of activity at home. At the office, he tried to make up for lost productivity. The evening routine was similarly chaotic: pick up the children from the babysitter; dinner; bath time; lay out tomorrow's clothes; get through the bedtime routine. Although stressful, Steve's frenzied schedule served as a welcome distraction from his heartbreak.

"It's when my kids are asleep and the house gets quiet that is hardest for me," Steve told the group. Often his thoughts drifted back to the final weeks of Catie's life. She had insisted on remaining at home to be with her children, but the heavy doses of pain medicine that she required left her sedated and unable to interact with them. When she refused the morphine so that she could stay awake, she felt miserable. Day after day, Steve watched helplessly as his wife suffered.

Toward the end of her life, Catie needed sedation nearly around the clock to remain comfortable. One evening, the hospice nurse noticed that her breaths were becoming shallower and told Steve that it would not be much longer. That night, Steve sat by her bedside and calmed her when she became distressed. Powerless to save his wife, this was all he could do. Sometime in the middle of the night, he drifted off to sleep. When he woke up a short while later, Catie had died.

Steve told the group he often wondered now whether she had woken up and needed his comfort. Was there a moment when she was alert and they could have said goodbye to each other? He had fallen asleep and would never know. "That's what I think about when I'm up late at night."

Several of the other men said that they, too, regretted how things had unfolded at the end of their wives' lives. Steve then shared an emotion that no one had yet spoken aloud in six months of group meetings. "I don't know if any of you guys have ever felt this way, but after Catie died, a part of me felt relieved that her suffering was over."

Steve's disclosure resonated immediately. Several of the men acknowledged similar feelings and thanked Steve for his candor. Up until this point, the discussions had focused on loss, sadness, and the stress of sole parenting. These conversations had been difficult, but we and the fathers had expected to deal with topics like those. This particular meeting represented something of a turning point for the group. Moving forward, the men would acknowledge other uncomfortable truths with increasing frequency: their marriages weren't perfect; at times, it was easier not having to negotiate two parenting styles; their desire for adult companionship had not died with their wives; and, in some ways, their tragedies were making them better people and better fathers.

The group now consisted of seven men who were clearly invested in each other. The meetings had evolved from a monthly gathering of what they called the "Dead Wives Club" to something much more. The men now trusted each other implicitly, and when they got together, nothing was off limits. This transformation both mirrored and promoted their own adaptations. Things were starting to get better.

PART II

Adaptation

8

The Good Enough Father

D onald Winnicott served in World War I and graduated from medical school before he reached the age of twenty-four. He accepted a position at London's Paddington Green Children's Hospital where he would work as a pediatrician for the next four decades. Early in his career, he became fascinated with theories of emotional development in infants and young children and subsequently trained to be a psychoanalyst. After observing thousands of interactions between young children and their mothers, Winnicott became convinced that the best way for parents to promote their children's psychological health was to help them navigate interpersonal relationships. Ultimately, he became one of the most influential psychoanalysts of the twentieth century.

Perhaps Winnicott's most enduring insight is the notion of the "good enough mother." His fundamental precept was that perfect parenting is neither possible nor desirable and that children benefit most when their caregivers do not immediately respond to each and every demand. He maintained that this approach teaches children to tolerate frustration and disappointment. Additionally, when children are allowed to fail in small and manageable ways, they learn to self-soothe and develop the competence to negotiate an imperfect world. Thus, the "good enough" parent is preferable to the "perfect" parent who aims (and inevitably fails) to meet his or her child's every desire.

Recognizing that most caregivers possess the necessary instincts and interpersonal resources to care for their children, Winnicott championed the notion of the "good enough mother" to promote more realistic parental expectations and remind caregivers that children can thrive with loving, competent but "imperfect" parents. This simple but profound idea would prove extremely valuable to the fathers in our group.

In Part II, we address four broad challenges that the seven men faced: assuming sole responsibility for all parenting and household duties; helping their children grieve the loss of their mothers; coping with their own grief; and taking steps to move forward with their lives. Every one of them found that the most pressing initial tasks were adapting to sole parenting and managing the home. The men attempted to compensate by trying to be the "perfect" father or, as several men saw it, both mother *and* father. In time, they would learn through their own limitations, and from discussions with each other, what Winnicott had observed decades earlier: that their children needed an attentive, thoughtful, and loving parent. Not a perfect one.

■

Joe's son, Christopher, was in the fifth grade when he took an interest in attending junior high at a prestigious math and science academy. The charter school specialized in his two favorite subjects and offered a more realistic chance of making the basketball team than he would have at his local middle school. Christopher pleaded with his father to let him apply. Joe was excited to see him take an interest in academics but worried about the logistics. The school was a thirty-minute drive from their home, offered no bus transportation, and there were no good carpool options from their neighborhood. Still, he agreed to submit an application.

Several months later, Christopher received his acceptance letter in the mail and immediately redoubled his lobbying efforts. Joe tried to figure out how he could incorporate two extra hours of drive time into his daily schedule. He almost had it worked out when he remembered that Christopher was also set on playing basketball. That would mean months of evening practices and weeknight games all over central North Carolina. Joe would have to bring Grace with him and they would not get home until well after her bedtime. In the end, that was the deal breaker. Christopher was deeply disappointed and for days, he kept pleading with his father to reconsider. Each time he said no, Joe felt like he was disappointing his son all over again. If Joy were still alive, this would have been easy. As a sole parent, Joe simply couldn't pull it off.

Over the ensuing weeks and months, Christopher seemed to adjust and he began to look forward to starting junior high with his neighborhood friends. When school started that Fall, he liked most of his teachers, was in the same classes as some of his friends, and even enjoyed riding the bus. Overall, the transition to junior high went well.

During one group meeting, Joe described how his feelings about the middle school decision had changed over time. "At first, it was another example of how I was letting my children down. They had already been through so much. Christopher not going to the school he wanted only added to the sense that nothing seemed fair. But, he's obviously done okay with it. He was upset, but he got over it. And as guilty as I felt, I'm past it now, too. All in all, it wasn't the disaster that I anticipated."

Joe's story provided a perfect opportunity for us to tell the group about Donald Winnicott. Joe had found his own way toward being a "good enough" father, and came to realize that he didn't have to be perfect for his children to be all right. In time, his ability to adapt in this way extended to other parenting demands, including a more relaxed attitude about Grace's morning hair routine.

Russ had a different fear about providing for his children. As the only father in the group without a daughter, Russ was worried about the lack of a female presence for his two sons, Michael and Aaron. He knew they were missing their mother's nurturing manner and compensated by going easy on them.

One weekend when Russ's sister was visiting from out of town they went to watch Michael play hockey. Michael was a talented player, and at six feet tall and nearly two-hundred pounds, had the potential to dominate on the ice. But despite the coach's repeated pleas for more physical play, Michael shied away from making contact. As Russ's sister watched her nephew play, she noted his timidity and said something to her brother. Russ quickly told her not to mention it after the game. "Seriously, don't say anything to him about it. I don't want to hurt his feelings."

Later that afternoon, they were talking in the kitchen when Russ's nine-year-old son, Aaron, ran in through the front door. Clutching his leg, he tearfully described how he hurt his knee while playing outside. Russ picked him up, placed him in his lap, and gently rocked him. After several minutes, Aaron settled down and ran back outside to play with his friends.

When Russ tried to resume the conversation with his sister, she stopped him mid-sentence and told him what she had been thinking since the hockey game earlier in the day, "I have to say it: You are babying those boys." She understood they needed some extra TLC after losing their Mom, but thought Russ was going too far. "You know, you're not doing them any favors by coddling them all the time."

At the next group meeting, Russ shared his reaction to his sister's comments. "Honestly, I was a little pissed at first. You know, I'm doing the best I can, and she's basically calling me out for being too soft."

"For me, it's been the opposite problem," Neill said. He had always been the primary disciplinarian and sometimes needed Deanna to buffer his temper when the children misbehaved. Neill was often quick to assign blame or hand down overly strict punishments. One time, years earlier, he was ready to ground the kids for a full week for forgetting to take out the trash. Deanna intervened and calmly delivered her standard line: "Okay, let's think about this for a second." Together, they arrived at a more even-handed response.

Without Deanna, and worn down by the relentless fatigue of being a sole parent, Neill struggled to manage his reactions. One afternoon, his teenage son, Jack, played a rather harmless trick on his little brother, Richard, sending him on a wild goose chase to find something that didn't exist. After realizing he had been pranked, Richard came running to his father. On his best day, Neill would have helped them work it out or simply told his oldest son to apologize. But Neill hadn't seen one of his best days since Deanna had died.

He yelled for Jack to come to the living room. "As I was sitting there waiting for him, I could practically hear Deanna telling me 'take a minute, think it through.' But it was too late." He told Jack that he was fed up with this kind of behavior and he grounded him for two weeks: no television, no video games, and no phone. When Jack began to protest, Neill told him that he didn't want to hear any excuses and to go to his room.

Almost instantly, Neill regretted his actions. "I hadn't even given my son the chance to explain. And two weeks was too harsh. I mean, I knew that."

Emotional warmth and consistent discipline are two cornerstones of good parenting that take on even more importance in households where one parent has died. A nurturing, yet structured and predictable environment, can buffer the chaos that a child who has lost a mother or father experiences. Both Russ and Neill wanted desperately to get it right for their kids. Providing both comfort and discipline was a priority for all the fathers, and the support group provided a perfect forum to share their problem-solving strategies.

Russ had bristled at his sister's comment but it prompted him to take stock of how things had changed between him and his sons. He soon realized that his sister had a point. "I think for a while, I was parenting out of guilt, trying to make up for the fact that they lost their Mom. I thought back to the rules that Kelley left for me and kind of knew I wasn't doing right by my boys." He challenged Michael to be more physical in the rink. He remained loving with both boys but was careful not to coddle. He assigned them more chores around the house and resumed his previous style of discipline.

In Neill's case, he saw the need for a course correction right away. After cooling off for several minutes, he knocked on Jack's bedroom door and asked to talk. Neill made it clear that he expected less teasing around the house but acknowledged that he had overreacted. He explained that adults don't always get it right the first time and gave his son a much lighter punishment. In the end, Neill expressed a level of humility and openness that he had rarely shared with his children.

"You know, that's not my usual style. I don't like to undermine my own authority as a parent or have my kids see me as a pushover. But it was important for me to be fair. It wasn't easy, but I think I ended up handling it pretty well."

Karl pointed out the difference in how Neill responded this time compared to the earlier crisis with his daughter. "Remember when you had that situation around the first anniversary of Deanna's death? You and Julie had both dug in your heels for days. It was one of first times we'd all met as a group, and you came in here feeling completely lost and basically asking to be told how and what to do. Compare that to now. You handled this one much faster and on your own. *That* is progress."

Karl had been struggling with his own recalibration at home. Before she got sick, his wife, Susan, had handled the weekly meal planning and did most of the cooking. After her death, he usually ordered out for dinner or heated up one of the dishes that friends had packed in his freezer. Karl did little grocery shopping other than to buy things like milk, cereal, and items his children could pack for their lunches. This continued for about six months until it struck him as unsustainable. At dinner one night, Karl said to his children, "We can't keep eating like this. It's not particularly healthy and it's too expensive. We need to start planning our meals better." His teenage daughter, Melanie, volunteered to help. Karl agreed, grateful to have one less thing to manage on his own.

For a while, the new arrangement worked well. But soon, the disagreements began: which groceries to buy, what dinners to cook, when to eat. One evening as they were cleaning up from dinner, Karl told the children that he had decided to renovate the kitchen. When Melanie started to offer suggestions, Karl said he had already ordered the new cabinets and countertops. Clearly offended that her father had made these decisions unilaterally, she told him that he really should have asked for her opinion first.

For Karl, this moment was a turning point. "I realized right then and there just how blurred the line between *parent* and *child* had become. I'm the parent and these are my decisions. More importantly, I don't want my daughter feeling like she needs to take the place of her mother. That's not fair to her.

"It was my own doing. I started to parent much differently after Susan died. I'm normally pretty firm on the importance of the family hierarchy, but I let things slide—mostly for convenience, but also because I felt bad for my kids. Somewhere along the way, I allowed my daughter to slip into the role of 'Junior Mom.'"

Starting with meal-planning responsibilities, Karl began to clarify his role in the home and those of his children. The process was not always smooth and he met some resistance along the way. What mattered most was that Karl was thoughtful and intentional about parenting in a way he felt was best for his children. In this case, the best approach meant not giving his daughter as much input as she wanted. As Donald Winnicott may have noted himself, his children didn't need him to be a perfect father, only a good enough one.

■

The concept of the "good enough father" struck a chord with the men for two reasons. First, it reinforced one of our repeated messages to the fathers: children need both structure and clear limit setting. Although the impulse to relax the rules following Mom's death was understandable, it was not what their children needed. Second, the "good enough" idea reassured the fathers that their parenting missteps would not necessarily and irrevocably harm their children. The men found this second idea, in particular, a relief because it gave them permission to take risks and make some mistakes. Something else was happening too. They were beginning to experience and share with each other some outright "parenting victories." These small but meaningful successes gave them confidence that they could pull off this whole "sole father thing."

For Dan, being a sole father meant having to confront his lifelong fear of being scrutinized by others. When Sarah was alive, she was the parent who interacted with their children's teachers and school guidance counselors, though Dan went along to all the meetings. She arranged the parent-teacher conferences, chaperoned field trips, and volunteered for end-of-year class parties. The front office called her when one of the children was sick or forgot to bring money for lunch. Dan was an active and involved father, but he had been grateful that Sarah took the lead managing all school matters.

Months after Sarah died, the school called Dan in because one of his children was struggling academically. Heading into the first meeting without Sarah, Dan's anxiety spiked. Not only did he feel pressure to advocate for his child's academic needs, but he was self-conscious about what the school personnel would think of him. Would they see him as a less capable parent than Sarah? What if he was unable to answer questions about his child's previous educational plans? Would they look at him and think "poor guy . . . he has no clue"?

As he had done the evening he attended his first support group meeting, Dan made it through the appointment despite his anxiety. He listened attentively, didn't make any egregious errors, and advocated capably for his child. If any of the teachers questioned his parenting competence, he hadn't noticed.

Dan shared his success with the group. "That may not be a big deal to most people—taking the lead in a school meeting—but that's something I never had to do when Sarah was alive. I was always the silent wingman. And until I actually did it by myself, I didn't know that I could. Even though I still feel like I'm dropping a lot of balls, it feels good to make a solid play every now and then."

As the father with the youngest children, one of Steve's first big challenges was helping his children enjoy Christmas without their mother. It had always been Catie's favorite holiday growing up as a child and once she had children of her own, her enthusiasm reached new heights. She decorated their home in red and green, dressed the kids in matching outfits for pictures with Santa, and prepared the same foods and desserts she ate as a girl. Steve, on the other hand, approached the holiday season with far less fervor, content to leave the fuss to others.

Now, leading up to his first Christmas as a sole father, Steve had a decision to make: keep up the traditions Catie had created or scale things down. Even though he preferred to keep the holidays as simple as possible, Steve knew he had little choice. He put up a tree and decorated it with the kids, took them to the nearest mall to take pictures with Santa, and drove them all over town to look at the Christmas lights.

"We talked about Catie on Christmas morning and that was tough. It felt weird to be celebrating without her. There's no question that my version of Christmas wasn't nearly as elaborate as what Catie had always accomplished. But overall, I think I did a good job and my kids were just fine. So, I'm glad I went through all the holiday fuss."

One of Bruce's motivations to be a good father was fueled by a childhood memory of an elementary school classmate whose father had died suddenly. While not best friends, Bruce and this child had played at each other's homes and even had an occasional sleepover. But, after his friend's father died, Bruce was afraid to go to the boy's home, which suddenly felt haunted. He made up excuses to avoid going to the house and absolutely refused invitations to spend the night. In time, their friendship dissolved.

Bruce feared that his children's friends might have the same reaction and was determined that his home would not be viewed as a place to avoid. When one of his daughters asked to have a slumber party for her birthday, Bruce wanted to make it as fun (and normal) as possible. He told her to invite as many guests as she wanted. She named twelve. "Perfect! Let's go big—the more, the merrier." Not to be left out of the fun, his other two daughters wanted their friends to sleep over as well. "No problem! Let's do it." In the end, Bruce had agreed to host a sleepover for eighteen girls.

The plan was to take them out for dinner and then come back home to watch a movie. Bruce reserved the largest table at a local pizza restaurant and recruited his in-laws to help with transportation. After dinner, Bruce led the girls down the street to the ice cream shop. On the way, he called out songs from his camp counselor days and the girls responded in unison. Onlookers waved and cars honked at the sight of this large pack of young girls singing and skipping down the street. Back at home, Bruce managed to get everyone to bed at a reasonable hour.

For Bruce, the evening was a revelation. He had hosted a sleepover of massive proportions, and his daughters' friends experienced his home as fun and accessible. He also felt confident, for the first time since Lisa died, that he could manage on his own. For a moment, he even had the audacity to believe that he had done something not even Lisa could have pulled off. But only for a moment.

9

A Child's Grief

Several months after Catie died, Steve asked his sister-in-law to watch his daughters for a few hours so he could spend time with his six-year-old son. David seemed to be doing well but Steve sensed he needed a little one-on-one time with his Dad. They spent the morning together cooking breakfast, playing outside, and building Legos at the kitchen table. David loved having his father's undivided attention. After they had been playing for a few minutes, Steve asked him how much he thought about his mother.

"I still feel bad about what I did—about how I made Mommy die."

"Wait, what?"

"Because of when I hurt Mommy. Remember? That day she came home from the hospital and I hurt her real bad."

"That day" had occurred nearly two years earlier. Excited to finally have his mother back home, David jumped into her arms and gave her a big hug. Catie winced and immediately grabbed her right shoulder, which was still tender from surgery and radiation. David immediately let go and backed away. His mother, now grimacing, tried to take deep breaths to ease the pain. After a few minutes, she told him that she was okay but that he needed to be gentler with her.

Steve had not thought about the incident since the day it happened. Considering all he and his family had been through, it had barely registered in his memory. Sitting at the kitchen table, he asked his son what he remembered. David talked about how he made his mother sick by hugging her too hard. Since he had made her sick, he was the reason she died.

"Buddy, no. No, no, no. That's not it at all." Realizing that his son had been thinking this way for almost two years made Steve nauseous. He placed his hands on David's shoulders and looked him in the eyes, making sure he had his full attention. He explained that the hug had absolutely nothing to do with his mother dying. "You and your sisters were the reasons that Mommy lived as long as she did. She took all those yucky medicines because she wanted to be with you guys so much."

David listened and seemed to accept what his father was telling him. Still, Steve made him repeat back in his own words that the hug had not caused his mother's illness and death. In the coming weeks, he would check in with David several more times and only let it go when he was convinced that his son no longer felt responsible.

"It's hard enough to lose your Mom, but to think it's your fault . . . I still can't believe that my son carried that around for so long. Thank goodness that he happened to mention it. Otherwise, he would still think that he caused his mother's death—and I wouldn't have had any idea."

"That's kind of the problem, right?" Russ said. "It's hard to know what your kids are thinking. My boys almost always look like they're doing fine. You know, it's not like they are going to walk up to me and say, 'Hey Dad, I've noticed that I haven't quite been myself lately—can we sit down and talk about Mom?' It just doesn't happen like that."

Russ knew all too well that a child's grief isn't always expressed through words. He was at work one afternoon when the assistant principal at his youngest son's elementary school called to say that Aaron had been in a fight on the playground. When he got home that evening, Russ asked what had happened, but all his son said was "I don't know."

The next morning, Russ took Aaron to school to meet with his third grade teacher. When pressed for an explanation, Aaron's eyes filled with tears as he described what led him to bloody a classmate's nose. "He said the reason I couldn't play basketball was because I didn't have a Mom." This wasn't the first time he had been teased, Aaron said, just the first time he had fought back. When asked why he had not told his teachers, Aaron said that he didn't want to be a baby and was afraid of being singled out in front of the class.

The school meeting provided Russ with a rare window into his son's grief. He realized that for Aaron, it was more than feeling sad or missing his mother. It meant worrying that his friends saw him as "different," being ashamed that he didn't have a mother, and feeling not as tough as his older brother. With a deeper understanding of what Aaron was going through, Russ redoubled his efforts to support his son. He arranged regular meetings with the school counselor and made sure to check in with him more frequently.

"My boys are almost five years apart and are very different kids, so it makes sense that they would handle things in their own way. Now when I check in with Aaron, I make sure it's just the two of us. That way he doesn't have to act all tough in front of his big brother. But even then, I never *really* know what either of them are thinking or how they're actually doing. I want to ask, but I worry that if I bring it up too often or in the wrong way, they'll shut down."

Knowing when to force the issue and when to lay back was particularly challenging for the fathers with teenagers. Neill had noticed for several weeks that his son was irritable and less engaged with the family. Each time Neill asked if something was bothering him, Jack insisted he was fine.

One morning, Neill reminded all of his children to finish their weekend chores. Jack rolled his eyes and let out an audible groan.

"All right, that's it. We need to talk. Son, what is going on?" Jack said it was nothing and started to walk off. This time, Neill insisted on an explanation.

"Is it something at school?"

"No."

"Something going on with your friends?"

"No."

"Does it have anything do to with your Mom?"

Jack said nothing and stared at the ground.

Neill put his arm around his son. "You know, it's normal to feel sad ab—"

"You don't get it," Jack interrupted, looking directly at his father. "I'm not sad. I'm *mad*."

"Okay. Look, what happened to Mom wasn't fair."

"You don't understand. I'm not even mad about what you think. I'm mad at *you*." Jack then unloaded what he had kept inside for over a year. Why wasn't he allowed to visit Mom in the hospital? How come nobody told him that she was going to die? Why didn't he get the chance to say goodbye? "It's like she just went to the hospital one day and I then never got to see her again. You didn't let me!"

Neill was stunned. He calmly explained that hospital policy didn't allow children to visit the intensive care unit. He told Jack that he, himself, had thought Deanna was going to be fine right up until the night she died. The plan was to have everyone visit once she returned to her regular hospital room.

"But, you're right . . . you're absolutely right. I should have found a way to make sure you got to see Mom . . . or at least given you that choice. I don't really know what else to say. I'm sorry."

Jack's tone softened. "So, like, what even happened at the hospital? I mean, how did it get so bad?"

"Well . . . what exactly do you want to know?"

"Everything."

The only other time Neill had recounted the details of the final two weeks of his wife's life had been when he introduced himself to the group. This time, his son desperately needed to know what had happened to his mother. Neill explained that Deanna's symptoms didn't seem serious at first, that the doctors did not identify the infection until it was too late, and that his Mom was unconscious but comfortable at the end.

When Jack asked questions, Neill answered them honestly and as best he could. Their conversation lasted a full three hours.

■

Every child grieves differently. As with adults, there are no predictable phases, and the expression of grief can include a broad range of emotions and behaviors. The extensive body of literature on childhood grief does, however, offer insights into developmental considerations that affect how a child responds to the loss of a parent. The fathers' stories highlight the most important findings from this research.

To some extent, a child's age and developmental level determine his or her grief experience. Preschoolers have a very limited understanding of death. They often cannot grasp that death is irreversible, which may lead to repeated questions about when Mommy is coming home. Steve's son demonstrated the kind of magical thinking—the mistaken belief that two unconnected events are causally related—often seen in young children. In contrast, Neill's teenage son could fully comprehend the permanence of death. Jack's struggle was to construct a coherent story about his mother's death so that he could better understand how and why his life had changed so drastically. A key developmental task of adolescence is forging a level of independence from caregivers, a process that can be profoundly complicated by losing a parent.

Social considerations also shape how children, especially older children and adolescents, express grief. This was evident with Russ's son, whose self-consciousness about his classmates' teasing kept him from telling his father about it. The desire to get peer approval and not stand out as "different" may contribute to a child's reluctance to speak openly about his or her grief.

Children often reveal their internal struggles through outward behaviors. Young children may lack the vocabulary or intellect to verbally express their thoughts and feelings. Articulating grief is tricky at any age and threatens to elicit overwhelming feelings. A child may also worry about adding to his or her parent's sadness. Not surprisingly, children often respond with a stoic facade, refusal to talk, or insistence that they are doing all right.

The challenge for the fathers was determining whether or not to accept an "I'm fine" at face value. Most of the time, their children seemed to be coping well even if they weren't sharing very much of their inner world. At other times, however, an emotional outburst at home or an incident at school could only be interpreted as an expression of grief. The fathers learned to watch for patterns that persisted over time. Between the periodic parenting advice that we provided and the fathers' rapidly accumulating real world experiences, they generated a checklist of sorts for when things, in fact, were not "fine" with their children: isolation from friends; recurring nightmares; excessive clinginess; a drop in grades at school; changes in eating patterns; and weight fluctuations.

This new skill of pattern recognition was helpful, but it only got the fathers so far. Sole parenthood included multiple moving targets. When Steve sat down with his son to build Legos, he could not have anticipated that the morning's task would be to convince his son he was not responsible for his mother's death. When Neill told his children to finish their chores, he had not expected that he would need to have a three-hour talk with his teenage son to repair a year of resentment. The fathers had a crash course in the developmental aspects of grief as well as in their children's unique reactions to losing their mothers. Over time, each developed more sophisticated ways to respond to his children's grief.

Group discussions revealed that being emotionally available to help their children grieve sometimes came at a cost. Neill raised this point in reflecting on his marathon conversation with his son. "Obviously, he needed for me to tell him what happened with his mother. But, that was a tough three hours. The whole time I'm reliving those two weeks at the hospital: all the medical decisions that I had to make, the way Deanna looked when she was on that breathing machine, and how helpless I felt at the end. That was the hardest part about talking with my son. I could handle him being mad at me. But having to relive all those memories that I spend so much time trying not to think about? That was brutal."

Neill's disclosure resonated with the group. While the fathers and their children had each lost the same person, they were grieving different relationships and in different ways. Their grief trajectories did not always converge or progress at the same speed. The men came to recognize that the interplay between the processes of parental and child grieving was another factor that made being a widowed father so challenging.

■

Steve woke up one morning feeling even more exhausted than usual. He had trouble falling asleep the night before and had stayed up late watching television. He rolled out of bed and checked the time.

9:52.

Nine-fifty-two! The kids always woke him by seven o'clock at the latest. Steve ran into his youngest daughter's room only to find her crib empty. The other kids weren't in their beds either. He panicked and ran downstairs. There, he saw the silhouette of all three children sitting quietly on the couch watching cartoons.

Steve caught his breath and asked six-year-old David why he hadn't woken him up.

"I wanted to let you sleep. I know you're tired." David had gotten up early and quietly brought his sisters downstairs. He made them bowls of cereal, put in their favorite DVD, and told them to use their inside voices because Dad needed to sleep. Steve was touched by his son's kindness and initiative, but told David that, in the future, he should always get him up.

A while later, David came back with a question. "Dad, what should I do if I wake up in the morning and you're dead?"

"What?"

"Should I just get breakfast ready for the girls? But what if we run out of food?"

"Buddy, you don't have to worry about that. I'm fine, okay. I'm not going anywhere for a long time." Steve explained that just because something awful had happened to Mom, it did not mean that he was going to die, too.

"It's just that I can't drive to the grocery store. So if the food runs out, should I just go to the neighbors?"

Clearly, simple reassurances were not going to work. David needed a plan. So, Steve gave him one. "Okay. If you wake up one morning and I'm not alive, here's what you do: walk next door to Mr. and Mrs. Stanwick's house and tell them what happened. They will come over to take care of you and your sisters—and make you breakfast—until Grandma and Grandpa can get here." This explanation seemed to do the trick. David nodded, gave his father a quick hug, and went back to playing with his toys.

Steve was shaken by the exchange with his son and brought it to the group. "I just hate that he couldn't be reassured with a simple 'Don't worry, Dad is going to be fine.' That would be enough for most six-year-olds, right? Unfortunately, he knows that parents can die. I mean, that's just really sad."

Karl responded first. "My kids are older, but I see the same thing." Karl's brother had recently suffered a heart attack. He had survived, but it was a major scare for the entire family. In the weeks that followed, Karl noticed that his children seemed much more concerned with his well-being and safety than ever before. "Hey Dad, when do you see your doctor for your next check-up?" "Why don't you order a salad for dinner?" One time, his son was particularly blunt: "Remember, Dad, you're the only parent we have left."

Karl offered an analogy to the group. "Imagine being on a really small plane, the kind with one propeller on each wing. The first part of the flight is smooth and uneventful; nothing to worry about. Then suddenly, a loud explosion rocks the plane. You look out the window to see smoke billowing from one of the propellers. The pilot tells you that it's okay, that the plane can still fly. Besides, just because one propeller went out doesn't mean the other one will. That may be true, but this is your life at stake. For the rest of the flight, you're sure as hell going to be paying a lot of attention to the only propeller you have left.

"We're our kids' only propeller and they know nothing is guaranteed. One of the legacies of having lost your Mom is to be reminded of that possibility every day."

Their children's anxieties extended beyond fears of losing their remaining parent. Dan and his children were in upstate New York at a family reunion when he noticed that his daughter, Bethany, was crying. When he asked what was bothering her, she said that nobody at the reunion had said anything about her mother. "They're not even talking about her.

And nobody seems sad, like they're all back to living regular lives. It's like everyone is forgetting about Mom."

Dan explained that people were probably unsure how to bring it up and that no one had forgotten her mother. Bethany then confided what was really bothering her. "Sometimes I worry that I'm forgetting her, too. It's getting harder to remember what she sounded like." Dan simply hugged her as she cried.

After that, Dan began to recognize how little he and his children talked about Sarah. Like him, both his son and daughter were uncomfortable talking about their feelings and shied away from difficult conversations. As a family, they had turned inward in their grief and rarely talked about the mother and wife they had lost.

Dan realized he needed to change that. He started by mentioning Sarah more frequently in everyday conversations: when a certain song came on the car radio ("your Mom used to love this band"); when election season rolled around ("You know if your Mom were here, she would already have us signed up to volunteer"); and at the dinner table ("Mom always made the best lasagna"). At first, the children responded with silence and half-smiles. Even to Dan, it sometimes felt forced. But in time, mentioning Sarah started to feel normal and occasionally led to a sweet, shared memory.

Bethany's comment about forgetting her mother's voice gave Dan another idea. Underneath the television in the family room sat stacks of home videos of preschool graduations, little league games, birthday parties and family holidays, all untouched since before Sarah got sick. Dan knew that the videos would elicit tears, but he hoped that enough time had passed that they would bring back positive feelings as well. He suggested that they watch the tapes, and to his surprise, the children agreed.

Dan sat with Bethany on the couch while his son, Corey, stood off to the side—almost as if to watch from a safe distance. As expected, they all cried as they watched images from happier times, before cancer invaded their lives. After about ten minutes, Bethany needed to stop. Still, watching the videos—even briefly—was a step in the right direction, and for Dan, it felt like an important milestone.

Group meetings allowed the fathers to share strategies to help their children stay connected with their mothers. Bruce made sure to tell his children stories about Lisa that were often humorous, and some included slightly embarrassing things. "It's important to remember Lisa for who she was—not some sanitized version like what you would hear at a eulogy. I want my kids to remember her as a real person. I'm hoping that if I repeat these stories often enough, they'll be able to share them with their own children one day."

In time, Russ and his sons started visiting Kelley's gravesite more regularly. "At first, they didn't know how to act. There were a lot of quiet car rides to and from the cemetery. But I kept taking them and it's better now. We change out the flowers, sweep around the grave, and bring out the weed eater every now and then to keep it looking nice. Lately, we've even brought the football to throw around."

Joe had an enthusiastic partner in keeping Joy's memory alive. "Grace has no hesitation in talking about the elephant in the room. She brings Joy up at least once a day. Thankfully, most of her memories are happy ones. Sometimes she'll ask me to tell funny stories about her Mom. Her favorite is about what a terrible dancer her mother was; we used to joke that Joy danced like Elaine from *Seinfeld*. So, Grace will say things like 'Daddy, do the Elaine dance like Mommy did.' So, of course, I oblige and the kids get a kick out of it. That kind of thing has been good for our family."

10

The Ring Thing

The ancient Egyptians were the first to use a wedding ring as a symbol of love and fidelity. Bands were usually made from grass or hemp and worn on the fourth finger of the left hand, which was believed to include the vein that led directly to the heart. The circular shape of the ring—with no beginning and no end—represented eternal love.

Over the centuries, societies throughout the world adapted the tradition to fit their own cultures. It was once customary in the United States for only the bride to wear a ring, but this changed during and after the marriage boom that followed World War II. The number of men wearing wedding bands more than quadrupled, and today, double-ring marriage ceremonies are the norm.

None of the men in the group had anticipated that "until death do you part" would occur so early in his marriage. After their wives died, what their wedding rings symbolized, and what should be done with them, was far from clear.

One evening as the group settled in, Joe reached toward the center of the table to pick out his sub and bag of chips when one of us (Don) noticed something different about his left hand.

"Joe, you took off your ring."

All eyes turned to Joe's left hand. A strip of pale white skin that had been shielded from the sun for nearly twenty years circled the base of his fourth finger. Before that moment, the men had never discussed the subject of wedding rings.

The prospect of dating again had compelled Joe to make the change. "It's not that I'm interested in anyone in particular. In fact, even thinking about going out with someone right now is kind of overwhelming. But, damn, I don't want to be lonely for the rest of my life. I hope that someday I'll feel for someone else the way I felt for Joy." Joe took off his ring because he wanted to believe that one day that time would come.

He had waited until after his extended family's annual Labor Day picnic to remove his ring. Aunts and cousins had already started to pepper him with well-intentioned but tiring questions ("It's been six months now, how are you managing?") and offered platitudes that grated on him ("At least she's in a better place."). Joe had no interest in inviting a new line of interrogation about his dating plans.

Several days after the picnic, Joe explained his thinking to his three oldest children. He emphasized that while he would never be "over" their mother and was not yet ready to date, it was time to make this change. The children said that they understood and seemed to take it well. Later that night, sitting alone at the foot of his bed, and with a silent apology to Joy, Joe slipped off his ring.

"My ring represented a lot. It was a constant for the biggest moments that Joy and I shared, starting with the day we got married. But also when we bought our first house, when our kids were born, the day we sat in that doctor's office and were told she had cancer, the day she died. During all the good times and the worst moments, I was wearing that ring. I never really thought about it like that when I was married, but it all hit me when I was deciding to take it off.

"And it's not just the things that Joy and I did together. It's everything that she won't be a part of now. All the birthdays, holidays, vacations. Everything with the kids: seeing them graduate; watching them get married; growing old together and playing with our grandchildren. It just sucks that we'll never have that. Whenever I think about it, I feel sad for Joy—and sad for us. All that kind of came together when I took off my ring, like I was closing that chapter for good."

Joe's story sparked a surprisingly animated conversation among the men about what their rings meant to them and what their removal would signal to others. Like Joe, several other fathers worried about how their children would react. Some were apprehensive about the reactions of their in-laws (were they still in-laws?) and whether it would further strain an already altered relationship. Each father was aware that the absence of a ring would likely signal his readiness to date again. For Russ, that was the main reason for his reluctance. "There is so much on my plate right now, I cannot even imagine trying to date someone. I suppose that keeping my ring on makes that easier."

That evening's discussion would mark the beginning of what the men would call "Ring Watch." Over the next year, they looked for and commented on each other's ring status at each meeting.

Neill was in no hurry to take off his ring. After all, wearing it aligned perfectly with how he felt: that he and Deanna were *still married*. "I didn't choose to be single and she didn't choose to leave me." In many ways, Neill felt as loyal to her in death as he had when she was alive. The ring simply reflected his enduring commitment.

As the months passed and other fathers took off their rings, Neill's perspective began to shift. With the benefit of group discussion, he came to appreciate that his history with Deanna would not be diminished without his wedding band. Still, he tried to ease into post-ring life by wearing it during the day and taking it off when he slept. For two weeks, he placed his ring on the bedside table before falling asleep each night. In the morning, the first thing he did was put it back on.

One day, Neill was at work when he realized he had forgotten to put his ring back on before leaving home that morning. His first instinct was to rush home to retrieve it but he resisted the urge and made it through the rest of the day. The next day, Neill placed the ring in a box and stored it away for safe keeping.

Neill's equivocation about parting with this small but powerful symbol of his marriage mirrors the oscillation that is central to the Dual Process Model. At times, Neill was intently focused on his former life and identity as a married man. He missed Deanna dearly, still felt married, and kept longing for that state of mind. And then in the next moment, he was struck by what was true, right here, right now. He was single and needed to look ahead.

Bruce didn't think much about his ring for the first year after Lisa died. He had decided early on to leave it untouched until he was past the first anniversary of her death. He had so many adjustments to make; why add to the list if he did not have to? And by deciding to wait, Bruce gave himself a yearlong reprieve from having to think about it.

As the anniversary date approached, Bruce became preoccupied with painful memories of the final days of Lisa's life. For weeks, he relived what had happened exactly one year ago. His daughters were off at camp when the anniversary date arrived. He knew there was no way he could sit around the house all day by himself, so he and Lisa's brother went to the beach for the weekend. They watched old movies and college basketball games to stay distracted. For Bruce, it was more about getting through the day than honoring Lisa's memory, which was something he and the girls saved for her birthday.

With the anniversary behind him, Bruce's attention soon turned back to his ring. He briefly tried to convince himself that it was okay to continue wearing it. But in the end, he decided to stick to his plan.

"I had thought about putting my ring in the back corner of my dresser drawer," Bruce told the group. "But I hated the thought of being apart from it."

Bruce paused the story he was telling the group, reached into his shirt and pulled out a silver necklace holding his ring. "I know it's kind of a compromise. But walking around without it on my finger is a big enough adjustment for me right now. This way, I always have it with me."

Bruce's solution spoke to a larger challenge for all the fathers: how to balance feeling connected with their wives and their need to move forward. Perhaps more than any other example, removing their wedding rings epitomized this struggle.

Grief and bereavement professionals have long debated essentially the same question: Does maintaining an emotional connection with someone who has died facilitate healthy adjustment or hinder it? The predominant view in most Western cultures for much of the twentieth century was that "letting go of," "working through," or even severing these bonds was necessary to resolve grief. Bereaved spouses were encouraged to "say goodbye" so that they could adapt to lives without the person who died.

A challenge to this conventional wisdom came with the 1996 publication of *Continuing Bonds*. Dennis Klass, Phyllis Silverman, and Steven Nickman, all grief and bereavement researchers, argued in the book that preserving connections with deceased loved ones was fundamental to successful adaptation. They defined continuing bonds as those internalized aspects of a relationship that endure after a person dies, for example, strengthening memories by reminiscing about the person, retaining meaningful possessions, and establishing traditions like regular visits to the gravesite. Continuing bonds may also take the form of incorporating the loved one's value systems or even their style of dress.

The publication of *Continuing Bonds* sparked a number of new studies on the relationship between continued emotional connections and grief. Interestingly, the findings from nearly two decades of research paint a mixed picture, and it remains unclear whether staying strongly connected to the deceased predicts better or worse outcomes.

Bruce did not wait for the research community to reach a consensus to be convinced that wearing his necklace was not impeding his ability to move forward, at least not now. "Sometimes I feel that it's a little bit of cop out. But it's not as if it keeps me from doing anything I wouldn't otherwise be doing. For now, I just feel better having it on me.

Dan, who had yet to remove his ring, was curious. "How long do you plan on wearing it?"

"I don't know," Bruce answered. "If one day I re-marry, I can't imagine it would be a big hit with my future wife! Hopefully, I won't feel the need at that point."

While wedding rings were the most visible reflection of the men's ongoing attachment to their wives, they were far from the only ones. In countless small ways, the evidence of a shared life was everywhere: a joint bank account; mail addressed to both of them; untouched closets and still-cluttered bathroom counters. Each day brought another reminder, another set of decisions about holding on or letting go, looking back or moving forward, or doing both.

Increasingly, the men used group discussions to arrive at honest appraisals of whether they were staying connected with their wives in healthy or detrimental ways. At times, the group would encourage a father to make a specific change to help him move forward. At other times, the men saw that relinquishing those connections was neither desirable nor possible.

For several months, Russ remained the only father in the group still wearing his ring. One evening, he described having made several unsuccessful attempts to take it off. He still felt the tension between shedding his identity as Kelley's husband and accepting his new reality. But after talking about it with the others, Russ sensed a newfound confidence.

Before going to sleep that night, Russ took off his ring. The next morning, he thought for a moment about putting it back on, but left it on the nightstand and went to work. Within days, Russ barely noticed not wearing it.

The next group meeting began with the fathers catching up with each other as they started eating dinner. Before Russ could even grab a slice of pizza, Joe nodded in his direction. "No ring!"

Russ grinned and raised his left hand. "I actually haven't thought about it much the last couple of weeks. But I knew you guys would notice."

The importance of Ring Watch coming to an end was not lost on the fathers. In a rare departure from his usually reserved style, Dan stood up and raised his water bottle. "Here's to us. We're getting there—slowly but surely, we're getting there." The others picked up their drinks and toasted to what felt like an important milestone.

11

Last in Line

L eaders of a support group often debrief after each meeting. So, when we started the group for widowed fathers, we made a point of scheduling time for this practice, even though it would make long days even longer. We used these conversations to reflect on any new themes that emerged during the session, the interpersonal dynamics between the men, and any changes we needed to make to the group.

What neither of us anticipated was how moved we would be by these men and what they were building together. Month after month, as the two of us talked following each meeting, we marveled at the fathers' willingness to share their fears and vulnerabilities. Their authentic exchanges with each other belied the stereotype that men are reluctant to talk openly about their feelings. Each time a father articulated a concern or newly discovered insight, the others responded with honesty and compassion. They were becoming part of something larger than themselves.

We found this project as interesting and meaningful as any professional work either of us had ever done. It was also uncharted territory. Because no one had ever led a support group for widowed fathers whose wives died from cancer, there were no books, articles, or lectures to guide us as group leaders or to shed light on the unique challenges these men were facing. Like the fathers, we were participants in this experiment and were committed to giving it our best shot.

The group sessions generated plenty of painful, awkward moments during which we had little or no comfort to share. They also sparked moments of profound insight, inspiration, and humor. Our post-meeting discussions gave us a chance to compare notes and appreciate the progress of each man and the group as a whole. Returning home after each session, we would tell our wives how great the group was that evening. Once a month we each felt especially grateful that we could share these successes with our spouses.

During our debriefing session on the night "Ring Watch" ended, we sensed that the group was at an inflection point. Up until then, the conversations had been about the fathers' most immediate problems: managing day-to-day life as sole parents; helping their children adjust; and coping with their own grief. Having achieved a better command of life at home, and no longer wearing their wedding rings, the men were starting to shift their focus. Collectively, they seemed ready to take on something new, something more than just getting through each day.

It occurred to us that, by necessity, the men had been prioritizing their children's needs ahead of their own. Now, our job was to guide them toward better self-care. For most of the men, that work began with acknowledging how much they had neglected their own needs and well-being.

■

Karl tried to avoid traveling for the first couple of years after Susan died. When he did leave home, he relied on family or friends to stay with his children. As his children grew older and became more self-sufficient, arranging weekend sleepovers got easier and Karl decided to take some time for himself. He and some of his friends from college met for a long weekend in Colorado.

For the first time in years, Karl had some time to himself without parenting responsibilities and found it liberating. The kids were doing well back home and he enjoyed re-connecting with his college buddies. One day he and his friends decided to hike a 14,000-foot mountain. It was a beautiful Fall morning. The sun was warm and the crisp air was invigorating. A perfect day to spend outdoors.

The hike started out well, but before long, Karl became winded. He slowed his pace but continued to have trouble catching his breath. His sides began to cramp, and his legs felt heavy and weak. Several times, he stopped to rest but each break provided only a brief respite. When the climb steepened, Karl knew he was finished. He found a flat patch of dirt on the side of the trail, sat down, and slumped his head over his knees.

Karl was surprised at how out of shape he had become. He knew that he had gained weight but had not appreciated how far he had let himself go. With sweat dripping down his face and still out of breath, he recognized painfully that he was no longer the fit and healthy person he had once been. After resting for twenty minutes, Karl slowly walked down the trail and back to his car.

That miserable hike turned out to be just the motivation that Karl needed. The next morning at the airport terminal, he walked past the pizza stand and picked up a garden salad instead. Upon returning home, he committed to a healthier lifestyle. He put his newly discovered meal planning skills to use and made more nutritious dinners for himself and his children. He brought fruits and vegetables for snacks at work and avoided the vending machine. He went for evening walks, took the stairs rather than the elevator, and rejoined a local volleyball league.

The results were soon evident. Steve was the first in the group to notice. "Karl, you're looking a little trim these days. Have you lost weight?"

"As a matter of fact . . . ," Karl said, taking a faux bow in front of the group, "twenty-three pounds as of this morning, thank you very much." He shared the story of his Colorado hike months earlier and how much more confident he had felt since making the changes. "I wish that I had started getting in shape before now. But after Susan died, my physical fitness wasn't even on my radar. For a while, I could barely even think straight. Everything was about taking care of the kids, holding on to my job, keeping the trains running at home, all that kind of stuff. I didn't have the mental energy—much less the time—to focus on myself."

■

In 2009, George Bonanno, a clinical psychologist at Columbia University's Teachers College, published a provocative and compelling book, "*The Other Side of Sadness: What the New Science of Bereavement Tells Us About Life After Loss.*" Bonanno argued that contrary to conventional wisdom, most people actually cope well following the death of a loved one.

Unlike much of the bereavement literature, Bonanno based his conclusions on rigorous scientific methodology and hard data rather than theory and clinical impressions alone. His studies identified three common bereavement trajectories: *resiliency*, in which a person experiences relatively minor disruptions in daily life and returns to pre-loss functioning within several months; *recovery*, characterized by moderate-to-high levels of distress that gradually abates over the course of about a year; and *complicated or prolonged grief*, in which significant distress is experienced for years (similar to the *DSM-5*'s candidate diagnosis of "persistent complex bereavement-related disorder").

In a series of carefully conducted studies, Bonanno demonstrated that approximately half of bereaved people (45 to 60 percent) follow the resiliency pattern. Another 15 to 25 percent recover over the course of a year or so, and fewer still experience prolonged grief. Thus, Bonanno's data, somewhat unexpectedly and reassuringly, show that the most common grief response involves relatively short-lived psychological distress. Bonanno notes that even when people continue to grieve, most return to living productive lives relatively quickly. Furthermore, those who do respond to a major loss with a pattern of either resiliency or recovery usually do so without the assistance of grief counseling or psychotherapy.

Bonanno contends that people possess the innate ability to overcome adversity. He points out that if the normative response to grief was to be devastated by traumatic events and remain incapacitated for long periods of time, humans would never have survived as a species for millennia. We are, in a sense, hard-wired to adapt.

How then do we make sense of the fathers' protracted struggles after their wives died? Certainly, none of the seven men returned to their base-line functioning after just a few months. Both their distress and the level of disruption in their lives continued far longer than even Bonanno's "recovery" trajectory would predict. Were the fathers in our group (as well as most of the men who participated in our research study) outliers? Since it's so difficult to know what happens to most widowed fathers, we may have simply encountered a self-selected group of men who suffered from an unusually difficult bereavement. This is certainly a possibility and likely explains some of our observations. However, our strong instinct is that widowed fatherhood represents one of several types of unusually chal-lenging grief circumstances.

Interestingly, Bonanno's more recent work provides some clues as to why widowed fathers may be especially vulnerable to an extended adjust-ment period. In a 2015 study, Bonanno and colleagues identified several factors that predict prolonged grief in bereaved spouses, including: prior dependence on their spouses; difficulty relying on social support; and the belief that members of their support system do not understand what they are going through. While there were likely very few widowed fathers included in this study (two-thirds were women and the average age was over fifty), it is not hard to imagine how these three factors are particularly relevant for widowed fathers. Indeed, we heard variations on these themes repeatedly from the men in the group.

■

Karl found his inspiration on the side of a Colorado mountain. Joe's moment of clarity took place early one morning in a cemetery. As he had done many times since Joy died, he had awakened in the middle of the night. One time he felt particularly restless and couldn't fall back asleep.

After lying awake for nearly an hour, he got dressed, grabbed his car keys, and drove to the cemetery where Joy was buried.

Joe had visited the gravesite often, but usually with the children and always during the daytime. Most of the time, he was able to maintain his composure. On this occasion, kneeling beside his wife's headstone, alone and in the dark, Joe fell apart. He began to sob and beat the ground with his fists.

Just a couple of months earlier, Joe had felt more hopeful about the future. He had become more competent at home, had taken off his wedding ring, and had begun to feel that he could rebuild his life. But without an obvious trigger or explanation, Joe's sadness and feelings of ineptitude had returned. Now, he found himself distraught, lying on the ground in a graveyard at four o'clock in the morning.

Joe eventually caught his breath and turned his attention inward. He hardly recognized himself. No longer was he the productive, self-confident guy who was always on top of things. He felt stuck and wondered if he would ever really be okay again.

As the sun began to rise, Joe drove home to get his children ready for school. Along the way, he became preoccupied with thoughts about how he could feel better, be better. Later that night, after the kids were in bed, he sat down and outlined a plan to get himself back on track.

Joe picked thirteen goals and gave himself three months to achieve them. Some were straightforward and not directly related to his grief: lose fifteen pounds; exercise four days a week; organize his home office; read more books; finish remodeling the bathroom. Others were more difficult: embrace his shortcomings ("Think of failure as a step towards success"); write letters for his children to open after he died ("Tell them what I love about them and what I want for them in their lives"); take down the dozens of pictures of Joy he had put up after her funeral ("It's almost like putting them away will change my memories or my love for her. Silly, I know, but I'm not always rational."); clean out her closets, bathroom cabinets, and dresser drawers ("This one will be hard—it seems as if getting rid of her things confirms the end in a way that is more permanent than her dying").

Joe named his plan "90 Days to Me." Writing it down made it feel real and gave him a sense of hope that things could actually change. He also knew this plan would be hard to accomplish on his own, so he sent an email to a small group of his closest friends:

Dear friends,

I am writing to enlist your help. I am sure that it is quite obvious to you that I have not made it through the grieving process. I thought that I had, but I still think of me as "Joy & me." There exists a huge hole that I am not hoping to fill, but rather to heal in order for me to grow. To that end, I am embarking on a journey to attempt to untangle the "me" from that picture. At this point, you're probably wondering "what does Joe want from me now?"

You folks are my (& Joy's) closest and most trusted friends. Without you, I would never have been able to make it at all. I'm asking for your continued support and prayers. The other reason that I'm sharing this plan is for accountability. So, *please*, hold me accountable.

I have been thinking of some of the things on this list for a while and never got around to them because I was scared or thought they would be too painful. Others are what I need to do to move my life back out of the fire and into the frying pan (I think "normal" would be setting the bar too high).

I know some of this crap is mushy but I thought it was important to share my perspective and ask for your support. With all that has gone on with me, I know that I have been truly blessed to have people like you in my life.

Thanks,

Joe

Over the next several months, Joe worked steadily toward his goals. He made great progress in some areas, less in others. More importantly, having a plan helped him climb out of his rut.

Joe's personal improvement campaign coincided with the unmistakable shift we had noticed in the focus of group discussions. The men now talked less about the deaths of their wives and they voiced fewer self-criticisms about their shortcomings as parents. Instead, they spoke more frequently about their own wishes, needs, and desires. They saw with increasing clarity that not only their children but they, too, deserved more than just surviving their tragedies. They didn't have to be last in line every time.

12

Dating 2.0

When Lisa created her family rules shortly before her death, she wrote them for her three daughters. She wanted the girls to remain close and look out for each other during the difficult days that would lie ahead. However, Bruce realized immediately that Lisa's rules were meant for his benefit as well. The last rule was unambiguous:

Support Dad when he is ready to date. He is going to need it.

Lisa wanted Bruce to find happiness again and did her part to make that possible.

Early on, Bruce had no interest in dating and felt disloyal to Lisa for even wanting companionship. After the one-year anniversary of her death, and with Lisa's explicit approval, Bruce reached out to an old friend who had offered to set him up. A lunch date was scheduled for the following week.

As the date approached, Bruce began to doubt himself. That morning, he tried to stay busy around the office, but as lunchtime neared, he panicked. He hurried down the hallway toward the office of a co-worker with whom he had become close since Lisa's death.

"I can't go through with it!" Bruce said as he burst through the door.

"Whoa, what's going on?" his friend asked.

"I'm not ready for this. I don't know what the hell I was thinking. To go on an *actual* date!?! It's too soon."

"Okay, just calm down. Have a seat and we'll figure it out."

Bruce continued to pace around the room. "Seriously, how can I have lunch with another woman and act like it's okay. It isn't. I was with Lisa for almost twenty years. I don't want to be with anyone else."

"I thought that she wanted you to date again."

"I know, I know. But how am I supposed to act . . . what am I supposed to talk about the whole time? That's it. I'm not doing it."

Grabbing Bruce by the shoulders, his friend looked him in the eyes. "*Get yourself together, man!* I know this is hard, but you've got to calm down. Besides, it's just lunch, you'll be back in an hour. Come find me afterwards if you need to talk, but for now, you have to do this. Now go!"

Bruce settled down, walked to his car, and made the short drive to the restaurant downtown, not far from where he had proposed to Lisa years earlier. There, he spotted a woman seated at a table who fit the description his friend had given him. Bruce walked over and introduced himself. He was on a date.

■

The idea of dating again turned out to be more complicated than any of the men had anticipated. It represented a clear line of demarcation between their former identities as married men and the potential of sharing a future with someone new. As each man began to date, he wrestled with his own version of competing thoughts, emotions, and practical limitations.

At several key moments during the group's progression, we used the Dual Process Model as a way to help the fathers better understand aspects of their bereavement. We emphasized that healthy grieving typically requires oscillation between loss- and restoration-oriented stressors. Each time we invoked this framework, it made sense to the men, who expressed a collective sense of relief that they weren't "doing it wrong" by not graduating from a specific stage of grief.

The Dual Process Model was particularly enlightening with respect to the men's dating-related angst. The anticipation of going out with another woman triggered memories of their wives and a sense of longing for the intimacy that each couple had built over years of marriage. Several of the men felt intense guilt for wanting to be with women other than their wives. Women who looked different from their wives. Acted different. Women who were healthy. Looking forward was not possible without looking backward.

Dating also offered both the promise and challenge of restoration. Adaptation. Growth. However, unlike suddenly becoming a sole parent or having to help a child grieve, dating was optional. It was up to each of the men to decide if—and when—to move forward in this way.

In time, each of the fathers came to believe that dating would be good for them. As they did, group meetings served as a perfect venue to sort through all that came with being a recently widowed man on the dating scene. They often relied on humor to express feelings of self-doubt; being able to laugh at themselves was most therapeutic when laughing with those who understood.

Joe described his first foray into the dating world without nuance. "To be honest, it was a complete disaster." The evening had started off well enough as he and his date settled into comfortable conversation. Then, about halfway through dinner, Joe's date asked about his children. He told her about each of them, including how Grace was adjusting well to a mainstream first grade class. Then, without meaning to, Joe started to talk about Joy. He described how they met in college, bragged about her accomplishments at the district attorney's office, and reflected on what his family had lost when Joy died. By the time Joe realized what he had been talking about, tears were streaming down his face. It would be several long minutes before he was able to collect himself.

"So you have to picture it: here I am in the middle of this restaurant with this woman who I'd just met, and I'm sniffling, snorting, and wiping away tears. I look up, and she has this deer-in-the-headlights look on her face. It was *so* awkward for the rest of dinner. I finished eating as fast as I could and asked for the check early just to get it over with."

Steve couldn't pass on the chance to needle his friend. "So, when's the second date?"

Everyone around the table laughed, including Joe. "Yeah, I'm sure she thought I was a real catch. Nothing sexier than a man crying about his dead wife, right?

"The only piece of dating advice that I can give at this point is to have that first one be with someone you *don't* like. Kind of like a sacrificial lamb or something—because if you're like me, you're going to butcher it."

Neill listened intently to Joe's first date story. He, too, still became emotional when talking about Deanna and he could easily picture himself breaking down in the middle of a dinner. Some months later, when preparing to go on his first date, he recalled Joe's disaster as a reminder to avoid bringing up his late wife. As it turned out, Neill's first date featured Deanna for entirely different reasons.

"I swear, it wasn't ten minutes before she started asking all sorts of questions about Deanna. 'How long were you two married?' 'What was she like?' 'How did you guys decide on the names for your children?' 'What was the best vacation that you two went on together?' I couldn't believe it! Here I was trying my hardest *not* to think about Deanna, and it seemed like that's all she wanted to talk about!"

"So, did all those questions make you emotional?" Karl asked.

"Yeah, I was emotional all right, but not in a sad way. I was more annoyed than anything. Look, I'm sure she's a very nice person, but I don't know what made her think I would want to talk about my wife all night. I guess she was just trying to make conversation, but that's kind of weird, right?"

Joe suggested that perhaps she was nervous. "I mean, it can't be easy going out with any of us. We're all still hung up on our wives and trying to figure out how to do something we haven't done in a long time."

Dan was one of the last fathers in the group to start dating. His shy nature made it tough for him to meet new people. He was also uncertain about what Sarah would have thought. In contrast to the fathers who knew that their wives had wanted them to date again, he was among the men who had received no such encouragement or permission. Dan and Sarah had never discussed the subject. He now longed for the clarity and freedom that might have come from such a conversation.

To some extent, their discomfort about this uncertainty echoed how the fathers felt about countless other decisions they had to make on their own, like which middle school their child should attend or whether to remain in the same house. The men were now the sole arbiters of their futures. While they valued those times when they could be confident of their wives' opinions, they had decisions to make, with or without that guidance.

Eventually, Dan was ready to date again. A few of the other men had tried Internet dating services, and the relative anonymity of these sites appealed to Dan. He created an online profile and within a few weeks connected with someone who seemed like a good fit. They met for coffee the following week.

"I just never felt right the whole time, like I was just kind of emotionally numb. I had this detached feeling when talking with her, as if words were just coming out of my mouth. Toward the end, I started to come around a little. Then I just felt guilty, like I shouldn't be doing this, like I was being disloyal to Sarah. I was relieved when it was finally over."

Karl was curious. "Do you think it would have been easier if you had Sarah's blessing?"

"Probably. I think so. It would have helped with some of the guilt. But the whole thing still would have been hard, I'm sure.

"I'm still glad that I did it, though. No matter when I started dating, even if I waited years, there was always going to be a 'first time.' So, it's good to be over that hump."

■

For some of the men, the dating era had begun in earnest. Increasingly, first dates led to second and third dates. The group conversations shifted from sharing awful dating moments to processing the complexities of new relationships. Each father tried to be thoughtful about whether, when, and how to talk with his children about new women in their lives.

Neill got dramatically different input from two of his children. Long before he had serious thoughts of dating again, his oldest daughter approached him one day with a surprising suggestion: "Dad, maybe you should start seeing someone. It may make you less grumpy." Around the same time, his younger daughter, who was then nine years old, came running in his bedroom one night, crying that she had a nightmare about being forced to have a "new Mommy." Unprepared and still half asleep, Neill told her not to worry and assured her that would never happen.

Karl told a story that spoke to another source of ambivalence that all of the men shared. He had been seeing a woman named Nancy for months and was clearly growing closer to her. While they were at the movies one evening, Nancy suddenly fell to the ground and for several moments was unconscious. Karl dialed 911. As he followed the ambulance to the hospital, his thoughts immediately returned to when Susan was dying. Thankfully, Nancy's medical problems resolved quickly and she was discharged that same night.

At the next meeting, Karl told the group what had happened. This clearly was not just a typical "bad date" story. Instead, it was a stark reminder that someone he cared for could fall ill in an instant. Karl made a confession: "It sounds awful, but as concerned as I was about Nancy, I was just as worried about becoming a caregiver again. I'm not sure I have it in me right now and I can't risk putting myself or my kids through that." Soon after, Karl decided to end things with Nancy. Her medical issues were just one factor, but not a trivial consideration. To Karl's relief, the other men acknowledged having had precisely the same fear.

The men's efforts to integrate their home and dating lives became the most frequently discussed topic in group meetings. They shared their children's complaints about the lack of fairness: "My kids asked me why I get to choose a new wife, but they don't get to choose a new Mom." Complaints from the men were common as well: "I'm dying to get laid." Other discussions focused on how the men could foster relationships between their children and the women they were now dating. What were the interactions supposed to be like? Was this Dad's new friend or a stepmother candidate? The prospect of a blended family made the fathers' deliberations even more difficult.

Bruce offered an analogy that captured the complexities of dating as a widowed father. "Back when we were younger, figuring out the whole dating thing was like solving a jigsaw puzzle. Sometimes it seemed hard to figure out, but really it was just a matter of finding someone who you liked and who liked you back. Basically, was it the right fit? Now, with kids and after having lost our wives, it's like trying to solve a Rubik's Cube. There are so many sides and combinations to consider. You know that it's possible to figure it out, but damn, it's not easy."

After months of dating updates, the subject of marriage entered the conversation. The children's ages seemed to be an important consideration in this regard. The fathers with older kids were in no hurry to remarry. Waiting a few years until their children were adults seemed like an easier path than introducing a potential new mother figure. In contrast, the men with much younger children were facing a decade or longer before their kids would be grown. The men provided each other with invaluable guidance as they sorted out their feelings about the new women in their lives. Our role in these discussions was to leave the dating advice to the men. Instead, we focused on helping them consider what those relationships meant to them and their families.

■

For Steve, delaying a serious relationship until the youngest of his three children reached adulthood would mean going it alone for the next fifteen years. After Catie died, that notion didn't seem like such a bad thing to Steve. He had little interest in meeting someone new and was too busy to give it much thought. Friends offered to set him up, but he had neither the time nor the inclination to invest in a new relationship. Eventually, though, as with all the men in the group, he grew tired of being the third wheel when out with married friends and longed for someone to talk with in the evenings who was over the age of eight.

About a year and half after Catie died, a longtime family friend told Steve that he had the perfect match for him: a woman in her mid-thirties who was raising two young children on her own after her husband's death a year earlier. The only problem, the friend said, was that she lived in Utah, some two thousand miles away. That part didn't bother Steve but he didn't want to be set up with someone just because of a shared widowed status. His friend assured him that they had much more in common than that and told Steve how to contact her. "Just think about it. Her name is Annie."

A couple of days later, Steve wrote a short email that he hoped didn't sound too awkward. To his relief, Annie responded that same afternoon. They began corresponding and eventually set a time to talk on the phone. That first conversation flowed easily and two hours went by in what felt like just minutes.

Before long, Steve and Annie were chatting on a nightly basis and exploring the possibility of a long-distance relationship. When Steve and his children flew to Utah for a previously scheduled trip to visit relatives (much of Steve's extended family happened to live there), he and Annie picked a night to meet face-to-face for the first time. The evening went even better than Steve had hoped. They connected with each other just as well in person as they had on the phone. For the next six months, Steve and Annie took turns flying to Utah or North Carolina to see each other as often as two sole parents could manage.

Steve updated the group on his relationship. He was surprised that he had fallen in love again, something that had seemed unimaginable just a year earlier. He and Annie were now talking about getting married.

"There's more to it than just whether we want to get married—we do. It's also about what's best for our children. Annie is a great mother and I know my kids have really missed having a Mom. I think it would be a good thing for them."

"What do your kids think? How much have you told them about all this?" Bruce asked.

"Well, they know about her. They understand that we're friends, but not much else. Remember, they are still young. My girls have said before that they want a new Mommy. I can see them getting attached very quickly, so I wouldn't want to introduce them to Annie until we decide for sure to get married."

At a group meeting several months later, Steve announced what everyone knew was coming. "Well, it's official, guys. I'm getting married." Steve shared that he and Annie had met each other's children, and that all had gone smoothly. The other men offered their congratulations and said how happy they were for him, and how heartened they were that he had found love again.

Steve had another piece of news to share: this would be his last evening as a member of the group, and not just because he was getting remarried. He and Annie had decided to live in Utah, where he had been offered a university teaching job.

We all thanked Steve for being a part of the "original seven." Joe congratulated Steve on his graduation from the "Dead Wives Club" to the "Soon-to-Be Remarried Men with Children from a Previous Marriage Club." Each father said a heartfelt goodbye to Steve who promised to send pictures from his wedding and updates on his new life out West.

Steve's engagement and departure from the group took some time to process. The men had bonded over their shared status as widowed fathers going it alone. Steve hadn't been the only one who was surprised that things came together with Annie as seamlessly as they had. The remaining six fathers had just started to imagine what it might be like to build a new life with someone else. Now Steve had actually done it. Not too long ago, they had all struggled to part with their wedding rings. Now, one of them was about to put on a new one.

The following meeting began with a serious conversation about the future and how uncertain it all seemed to them. They had each weathered the first year or two and knew they could get by on their own if they had to. But what was supposed to happen next? Steve had been the first to leave the group. Who would be the last?

PART III

Reimagined Lives

13

Future Trajectories

Steve's departure from the group shook things up. To the rest of the men, it seemed as though he had sorted things out sooner and more fully than they had. They were genuinely happy for their friend but also wondered what his ability to commit to a new relationship meant about them. More than ever, the men questioned whether they were simply adjusting at their own slower pace or were, instead, spinning their wheels and unable to move forward.

For a brief period after Steve left, the men talked about remarriage as though it was the most obvious measure of resolved bereavement. This view was reinforced by their interactions outside of group meetings. When friends and relatives asked them if they were dating again, the men heard that question as a proxy for "Are you doing better yet?" If they could answer "yes," that felt like progress. By extension, it was tempting to think of remarriage as the main goal of their grief work.

The more the men processed Steve's departure and the complexities of committing themselves to someone new, the more they realized that marrying again was not the most important or even a necessary objective. Healing included far more than replacing their wedding bands.

Increasingly, the men wrestled with larger questions. What was most important to them now? What kind of fathers did they want to be? Were their jobs meaningful and, if not, could they risk changing careers? Each man had already confronted a radical disruption in his imagined life trajectory, a loss of the future he had thought would be his. The challenge now was as much about reimagining a future as it was about coming to terms with the past.

■

One evening after the group had been meeting for about two years, the conversation stalled as the men tried to articulate their hopes about the future. During that rare moment of silence around the table, I (Don) decided to share a personal story about how I moved forward after a very different kind of loss. I had not previously talked about my own family with the men. I had no firsthand knowledge of losing a spouse and carefully avoided any suggestion that I could relate to what they had experienced. Yet on this night, as the men struggled to picture the next chapters of their lives, I felt compelled to tell them about my son, Koby. I recounted a version of the following essay that I had written years earlier for the NPR program *This I Believe*:

> I believe in adaptation—that is, the same stimulus does not invariably elicit the same response over time.
>
> The first time I saw my son flap his arms, I nearly threw up. My son Koby was 2 at the time, and he and my wife and I were at an evening luau in Hawaii. Dancers emerged from the dark twirling torches to loud, rhythmic drumbeats. I thought it was exciting and so did Koby. He began to flap his arms—slowly, at first, and then with an intensity that mirrored the movement of the dancers.

In an instant, I was overwhelmed. I knew just enough about arm-flapping to know that it was characteristic of autism. I was confused, panicked and strangely preoccupied with the fear that I would never play tennis with my son as I had with my father. That one movement took on immediate, powerful and symbolic meaning: Something was terribly wrong with my boy.

Koby is 16 years old now. He lost his language, developed epilepsy and has struggled profoundly. We've all struggled, including Koby's little sister, Emma. But we've also adapted. Koby still flaps his arms and he's got the thick, muscular upper body one would expect after 14 years of isometric exercise. He's a sweet and beautiful boy, and together we've been on a journey into frightening and unknown territory. Like any fellow travelers, we've learned from each other and grown.

Koby's arm-flapping means something different to me now. It means that he's interested, tuned in and present in the moment.

That Koby has autism is old news at this point. We've grieved, survived and adapted. We've learned to be more patient, to celebrate more modest victories, and to connect with Koby whenever and however we can. Now, when Koby flaps, I'm happy for him and what it means about his engagement, not sickened by what it might mean for his and our futures.

Same stimulus, different response.

I believe that this lesson in adaptation has been one of Koby's greatest gifts to me, to our whole family. I've seen it as Emma's embarrassment over her brother's condition has faded and been replaced with compassion for those who struggle. And I've seen the influence of Koby's lesson in my own work, helping patients cope with illness and tragedy in their lives—like my patient who can finally celebrate her father's memory after years of debilitating grief that came with every anniversary of his death.

Last summer, Koby had a delirious romp in the ocean alongside Emma. Koby flapped his arms wildly in anticipation of each coming wave. Not quite the family beach day we had once envisioned, but a spectacular moment nonetheless.

Old heartbreak, new appreciation.

I believe that "reframing a problem" can help to overcome it. But adaptation is not the same as becoming tolerant of or inured to something. Adaptation allows for creative possibilities. Koby has adapted to us and we to him, and through this process our family has discovered deep and meaningful connections with each other—connections we never thought possible.

I wrote that piece in 2007, well before I moved to North Carolina and focused my work on the psychiatric care of patients with cancer. When Justin and I began the Single Fathers Due to Cancer project, I saw the parallels between my own experiences with Koby and key aspects of what the men in our group were going through.

To be clear, Koby didn't die. He is now twenty-five years old, robust, and still has great moments as well as plenty of rough stretches. What did die many years ago, however, was my fantasy about what our family life with Koby would be like. Reading together. Family dinners. Vacations. Woodworking. College. Grandchildren. And, yes, the next generation of father-son tennis matches.

The future is not promised to any of us and in that regard it is always fantasy. Even though I never experienced any of those imagined scenarios with Koby, I felt as though they were lost and I grieved for them. I am still grieving and my grief has left me broken in ways that can never be fixed. I have also worked hard to construct new imagined trajectories. Of course, none of these revised versions is guaranteed, either. They too are fantasies that may or may not unfold as planned.

The men appreciated my story about Koby and thanked me for sharing it with them. I sensed that they were relieved to hear from an expert that some losses take a long time, perhaps a lifetime, to process. They also seemed to embrace the notion of reinventing their lives rather than focusing only on repairing or compensating for what they had lost.

14

The Meaning of Life

Not long after Susan died, Karl traveled to Connecticut to attend a wedding. He anticipated some uncomfortable moments but made it through the ceremony without feeling too sad. The reception was much more difficult. Karl was sitting alone and nursing a drink when the deejay announced:

> *Listen up everybody. I need all the married couples to come out on the dance floor.*

A dozen or so couples came forward as the deejay explained the rules.

> *I want everyone to keep dancing until I call out the number of years that you've been married. Let's start with an easy one: take a seat if you've been married for less than four hours.*

The smiling bride and groom walked off the dance floor as their guests laughed and applauded.

Now, keep dancing if you've been married for five years or longer.

Several young couples took their seats.

Ten years . . . fifteen years.

Karl's heart sank. He and Susan would never reach that milestone. Their number, 14, was frozen in time.

The contest ended when an elderly couple who had been married for more than fifty years were the only dancers remaining. As the guests stood and clapped, Karl sat in silence and scanned the room. The contest winners were on a victory lap of hugs and high-fives. The newlyweds stood to the side of the dance floor staring deeply into each other's eyes. Karl was alone and Susan was dead. Nothing about this celebration felt relevant to him.

■

The focus of group meetings continued to evolve. In the beginning, the group was mostly a safe place for the fathers to share their grief and feel less alone. It quickly became a practical problem-solving get-together and over time matured into a forum to experiment with personal reinvention. The men and their children had experienced staggering pain that often struck them as completely meaningless. They related to Karl's experience at the wedding in that they also often felt alone, disconnected, and fundamentally confused about their new place in the world and whether it even mattered. Increasingly, the men would talk with each other about fate, bad luck, faith, and nothing less profound than the meaning of life itself.

Our approach to this development was to follow the men's lead and get philosophical. We explained that Karl's wedding reception moment was something of an existential crisis. That is, he was experiencing the profound distress someone feels when questioning the very meaning, value, or purpose of life. Several modern psychotherapies are based on the principles of the early existential philosophers Soren Kierkegaard, Jean-Paul Sartre, and Friedrich Nietzsche. We then told the men about an Austrian Jew and Holocaust survivor named Viktor Frankl whose life experiences and writings we thought would resonate with them as they tried to find meaning in their grief.

Frankl was born in the early 1900s and was raised in Vienna. A child prodigy, he possessed a fierce intellect and intense curiosity about both philosophy and psychiatry. Even before he graduated from high school, Frankl wrote an article on psychoanalysis and lectured about existential issues confronting mankind. He subsequently enrolled in medical school, trained in psychoanalysis, and was rapidly becoming a successful psychiatrist.

Then, on the precipice of World War II, Frankl's life changed dramatically. Nazi forces invaded his native Austria in 1938, and he was forced to abandon his private practice and take a job at the only hospital in Vienna that treated Jewish patients. When the Nazi regime closed that hospital several years later, Frankl knew he was in danger. The United States granted him a visa, but he felt duty-bound to remain with his elderly parents and allowed the visa to expire.

In the fall of 1942, the Nazis arrested Frankl, sent him to Theresienstadt "camp-ghetto," and tattooed his wrist with prisoner number 119,104. Here and in three other concentration camps, he endured hard labor and survived on a diet of stale bread and watered-down pea soup. The depravity of the camp and the cruelty his captors inflicted shocked him. Death was a constant specter. As the Nazis killed rising numbers of his fellow prisoners, Frankl had every reason to believe that his own death was imminent.

Before the war, Frankl had started writing a book about a new kind of psychotherapy centered on the idea that people want to find meaning in their lives. He had smuggled a working copy of his manuscript into the concentration camp, but a guard had confiscated and destroyed it. Separated from his family and fearing death, Frankl faced a tragic test of his own theory. Ultimately, what he discovered only strengthened his beliefs. Despite unimaginable misery, his love for his wife and his passion for his work gave him meaningful reasons to live. He vowed that if he regained his freedom, he would finish the book. He also imagined one day lecturing about his Holocaust experience and, in doing so, offering hope to others.

Frankl recognized a similar resolve in many of the other prisoners. Some were sustained by the hope of freedom, however faint, while others were determined to survive for the sake of their children. Frankl observed that even during moments of deepest despair, he and the others fared better when they could find some reason to persevere.

After the Allied Forces liberated his camp in April, 1945, Frankl returned to Vienna and an existence that bore little resemblance to his prior life. He learned that the Nazis had killed his wife, parents, and brother, and he fell into a deep depression. Work became his only comfort, and he meticulously reconstructed and finished the book that he had started before the war. He also began writing a new book about his Holocaust experience. Dictated in just nine days, it would become one of the most impactful literary works of the twentieth century.

Published in 1946 and originally titled *A Psychologist Experiences the Concentration Camp*, the book recounted excruciating details of life as a prisoner but went far beyond a retelling of Nazi atrocities. Frankl wrote beautifully about the critical importance of finding meaning in one's life, especially during times of greatest suffering. He had been powerless to change his circumstances in the concentration camps, but what he did control was how he responded to those circumstances. Frankl wrote that "unique opportunity lies in the way in which [someone] bears his burden." Suffering is unavoidable, but each of us can try to find meaning in that suffering.

Frankl's seminal work (subsequently retitled *Man's Search for Meaning*) has been published in dozens of languages and sold more than twelve million copies. In the updated edition, released in 1962, Frankl introduced more detail about his psychotherapeutic approach to help people identify purpose in their lives and behave in accordance with their values. Frankl believed that the inability to find meaning leads directly to "existential frustration" and emotional distress.

Contemporary clinicians and researchers have also developed meaning-centered psychotherapies for exceptionally challenging times. William Breitbart, MD, and his colleagues at Memorial Sloan Kettering Cancer Center designed an intervention based on Frankl's work to help bereaved parents. Their research shows that meaning-centered psychotherapy fosters a greater sense of hope and purpose for these parents.

Robert Neimeyer, PhD, a psychologist at the University of Memphis, employs a similar meaning-based approach. In Neimeyer's view, healthy adaptation after the death of a loved one depends, in part, on the mourner's ability to reconstruct a sense of purpose and incorporate the loss into their life narrative.

Breitbart, Neimeyer, and other leaders in the field consider it critical for the mourner to make some sense of why the loved one died and find benefits in the loss. Most of the research in this field has shown that finding meaning in these ways predicts better coping and adjustment for bereaved persons. Nonetheless, not all mourners search for meaning and among those who do, some search in vain. Still, the balance of evidence suggests that for most people, finding purpose in suffering helps them adapt.

What any one person finds meaningful is influenced in substantial ways by their circumstances and is likely to change over time. Neither Frankl nor any of the modern proponents of meaning-centered psychotherapy believes that there is universal meaning in life. Instead, people must determine for themselves what is most meaningful, purposeful, and important. For the men in the group, this search was about fatherhood above all else.

■

One afternoon, Russ was watching his youngest son, Aaron, play his final game of that year's little league football season. Toward the end of the game, Russ noticed two women walking up the bleacher steps in his direction. He recognized them as mothers of his son's teammates but had not met them before.

"We apologize if this is awkward," one of them said, "but we wanted to tell you how great you are with your son." They had seen Russ at every practice and game during the season and admired his connection with

Aaron. "It's just so nice to see how you support him after each game whether we win or lose. You two obviously have a great relationship."

The former Marine was taken aback. "Oh, okay. Well, thank you."

One of the women also had a request: "Is there any chance that you would be willing to talk with our husbands sometime? It doesn't need to be a big deal, but it would be great if you could talk with them about how to be more involved with the kids." When she suggested that he teach a class on parenting, Russ wondered if he was being pranked. But this wasn't a joke. Russ stammered for a moment before offering a non-committal "Sure."

As the women walked away, Russ tried to make sense of the unexpected interaction. He saw the irony of receiving praise for his parenting competence during one of his son's sporting events. Two years earlier, while at his older son's hockey game, Russ's sister had criticized him for being too soft with his boys. Since then, Russ focused on being both nurturer and disciplinarian. The afternoon at the football game was a clear indication of the strides he had made.

The women's gesture touched Russ deeply. Indeed, it was the best compliment that he could have received. Considering all that he and his boys had been through, being a good father was his top priority. Russ was discovering meaning in precisely the parenting activities that had caused so much angst after Kelley died.

■

Karl too found a way forward through a realization connected with parenthood. He, like Russ, had come to appreciate how being a father added meaning to his life in a different way than it had when Susan was alive.

Several years after the wedding in Connecticut, Karl attended a funeral for a cousin who had died unexpectedly. Enough time had passed since Susan's death that he could sit through such family events without feeling overwhelmed. During the service, Karl listened as several family members shared poignant stories about his cousin's character and legacy. Then, the pastor spoke. His message to the congregation was that a relationship with someone does not end when they die. "In fact," he said, "not only does that relationship continue, but it changes over time."

Speaking directly to the children of Karl's cousin, who were seated in the front row, the pastor added, "How you think about your father years from now will be different. One day, when you have children of your own, you will have a different appreciation of him. For each of you, your relationship with your Dad will evolve, and it can be what you need it to be at different times in your life. That's a good thing."

Karl immediately thought of Susan and how his views of their relationship had shifted since her death. Like any marriage, theirs had not been perfect. In the immediate aftermath of his loss, Karl had glossed over their marital warts. In time, he felt less compelled to canonize his relationship with Susan, and developed a more realistic perspective on what each of them brought to the marriage and on what they meant to each other.

Karl also saw Susan's parenting strengths in a new light. He now recognized that their different styles had complemented each other well and he made a conscious decision to adopt some of Susan's parenting approaches as his own. In that respect and others, Susan remained a presence for Karl and the children.

For the second time since Susan died, Karl found himself lost in thought at a family event. But in sharp contrast to the panic and isolation that he felt at the wedding, the funeral brought him a sense of calm, connection, and hope for the future.

15

Posttraumatic Growth

An old clinical pearl passed down by mental health professionals holds that patients can be the "last to know" that they are getting better. Clinicians often notice improvements in mood, energy, and outlook before the patient appreciates these changes. We saw a variation of this phenomenon in the fathers. The men frequently pointed out to one another areas of progress and moments of growth even when they were unable to see similar changes in themselves.

In the months following Deanna's death, Neill struggled to hold on to a career in the private healthcare industry that he had spent years building. Traveling several nights a week for work had been manageable when Deanna was alive. However, as the sole parent of four children, Neill knew he wouldn't be able to maintain this schedule.

Neill met with his supervisors and asked if he could reduce the number of days he had to be on the road. Unfortunately, the job required a minimum amount of travel that was simply too much for him to manage and he reluctantly resigned. Neill couldn't bring himself to conduct an extensive job search in the rapidly changing healthcare field. Instead, he reached out to a friend who needed help managing local apartment complexes. The job wasn't glamorous and paid less than what Neill had been earning but it offered flexible hours, required no travel, and gave him the time he needed to care for his children.

Even as Neill began his new job, his focus remained on his family. When either of his younger children was too sick to go to school, he remained at home for the day. If he stayed up late helping his older children complete a science project or term paper, he went to work the next morning more exhausted than usual. Despite feeling physically and emotionally drained, Neill discovered something unexpected: He was growing closer to his children.

He and his teenage son, Jack, were communicating better than ever. Their long and difficult conversation about the circumstances leading up to Deanna's death had been a turning point in their relationship. Neill's two youngest children were now physically affectionate with him in ways that they had once reserved for their mother. But the changes in his relationship with Julie surprised Neill the most. As a fifteen-year-old, she had insisted on spending the first anniversary of her mother's death with her friends rather than with her family. Now, as a college freshman, Julie called Neill nearly every day to tell him about her classes and new friends she had made. She clearly missed her father and Neill felt great about that.

At a group meeting nearly two years after Deanna' death, Karl asked Neill if he still felt that the wrong parent died. Neill thought for a moment before answering. "I suppose that a part of me will always feel that way. But I don't think about it the same way now."

"What changed?"

"Well, lots of things. I'm around my kids so much more than I was before Deanna died. And when I'm with them, I'm really *with* them. My relationship with each of my children is better. I'm not saying that we don't still have our moments but, overall, we are much closer than before."

"So, does that mean you no longer think they ended up with the wrong parent?"

"Listen, you guys have heard me talk about how Deanna was such a fantastic mother. The kids were so attached to her and they always went to her first for everything. Now that I'm the go-to parent, that's how they see me. So, I guess that I don't see it as a comparison anymore. The reality is that there's just one parent left. Me. I'm doing the best I can and I'm just glad that my kids and I are tighter."

"I feel the same way." Bruce replied. "My girls and I wouldn't be as close if Lisa were still alive. It's ironic that we feel more connected to our kids *because* our wives died. I never would have been the one to talk with them about all the 'female stuff.' Now? I'm practically an expert on periods, tampons, training bras, you name it. At first, I thought there was no way that I could have those conversations. But I had to and it's changed how we communicate as a family. I desperately hate being a widower but I love that I've grown closer with my kids as a result."

Neill asked Bruce, "Do you ever worry about how people will react when you say stuff like that? I don't know, almost as if it sounds like you're glad that Lisa died."

"I used to worry about that, for sure. Each time I would mention something being better now compared to how it used to be, I felt like I needed to begin by saying, 'Of course, I would have given anything if Lisa hadn't died, but. . . .'"

"Exactly. I'm the same way," Neill said.

"I've stopped doing that, though," Bruce added. "People get it. They understand what I'm saying. And if they don't . . . well, that's not my problem. I don't need to apologize because some good has come from my nightmare. None of us do."

The exchange between Neill and Bruce was an explicit acknowledgment of unexpected growth after the deaths of their wives. It represented a shift in how the men would talk with each other about their experiences. Instead of merely surviving their tragedies, they were, in some ways, growing in surprising ways. The group started sharing other stories of getting "better": improved planning and organizational skills; newfound creativity in the kitchen; deeper empathy for others who were struggling in one way or another; the courage to audition for a church play. We explained that these were all examples of posttraumatic growth and told them about the blossoming body of research on trauma-related benefits.

In the mid-1990s, Richard Tedeschi and John Calhoun, research psychologists at the University of North Carolina at Charlotte, introduced the term *posttraumatic growth*. In contrast to the familiar, long-established problem of post-traumatic stress disorder (PTSD), in which a traumatic event leads to physiological, mood, and behavioral symptoms, posttraumatic growth is the process by which people adjust, adapt, and even thrive after trauma.

PTSD and posttraumatic growth may seem like two ends of the same spectrum; however, research suggests that they are separate, if still related, responses to trauma. In fact, people who endure traumatic events often experience both distress and growth simultaneously or at different times.

Researchers have identified several ways in which a person may grow following a tragedy. Neill and Bruce demonstrated perhaps the most important change: improved interpersonal relationships. People may also feel more appreciation for things they once took for granted or find that they are open to new opportunities. They may develop a deeper understanding of their spirituality or feel stronger and more resilient than before.

Tedeschi and Calhoun have looked specifically at how posttraumatic growth occurs in the context of bereavement. They based their approach on the premise that people possess core sets of beliefs or assumptions that help them make sense of the world and predict how things are likely to unfold for them. These assumptions shape our interactions with those around us and differ as a function of personality factors, cultural norms, and our prior experiences.

The premature death of a loved one can profoundly challenge one's worldview. When we grieve the loss of an elderly grandmother, we may be very sad but are not shocked. Her death is in line with what we consider to be a full life. In contrast, when a young wife and mother dies, our belief system can be shattered.

This was precisely what Joe experienced after Joy died. He had always believed that, for the most part, the world was a fair place where good things tended to happen to good people. He wasn't naïve. Learning that his daughter had Down syndrome certainly challenged his assumptions about the fairness of life. Yet Joe could manage those feelings. His family was intact and they all celebrated when Grace was born. Joe's outlook on the world was shaken but not broken by his daughter's diagnosis.

Joy's death was different. He was crushed and the world no longer felt like a remotely fair place. Joy had been a loving wife and mother who devoted her career to serving society's less fortunate. She deserved better.

For a time after Joy's death, when Joe simply "didn't give a shit," he was unable to imagine a future filled with goodness, fun, and just rewards. Although he could not unlearn what his tragedy had taught him, in time his pessimism began to fade. He found some comfort in clichés that he had always considered trite. "Make every day count." "Life is fragile." "Take time to tell people that you love them." In some respects, Joe's "90 Days to Me" plan reflected a return to his earlier optimistic worldview but it was more than that. As he wrote that plan, he was forced to reconsider and revise what was and was not promised to him and his children.

Tedeschi and Calhoun argue that traumatic events set the stage for personal growth by compelling us to reevaluate our core beliefs. While this evaluative process inevitably entails emotional distress, that distress is precisely what drives posttraumatic growth. In that way, psychological growth is an active process. People must make deliberate reassessments before they can reconstruct a worldview that incorporates important aspects of the tragedy.

Group meetings helped the men think collectively about moving forward in a constructive manner. For some, simply participating in the group represented personal growth. This was most evident with Dan, who remained temperamentally uncomfortable in social situations but had become a key member of the group nonetheless.

One evening, we asked Dan to reflect on his participation. He cleared his throat. "Everyone here knows that I'm not exactly in my comfort zone being in front of groups of people—especially when talking about the kind of stuff we've discussed in here over the last couple of years. To be honest, I'm kind of amazed that I've stayed with it. But it's been good for me. I've had to consider things that I would have avoided thinking about—much less *talking* about—otherwise. I'm definitely more comfortable here, with you guys, than I would have expected."

In part because of his experience with the group, Dan viewed himself as more psychologically sturdy and resilient than before. He shared this newfound confidence with the group. "If I can make it through this, I can make it through anything. Each of us has had to deal with so much these last couple of years. But we've survived. And in some ways, we're better men for it."

■

The men seldom discussed matters of faith during group meetings. We neither encouraged nor discouraged this topic. Nonetheless, several of the fathers relied on their religious beliefs to understand and process their losses. And, like nearly everything else in the men's lives, those beliefs were affected by all they had been through.

Faith had been a constant thread throughout Bruce's life. He was raised by a Baptist minister, worked for a faith-based organization (the YMCA) since graduating from college, and had previously served two years as an elder in his church. When Lisa was alive, the entire family attended services every Sunday morning.

In the years before Lisa's illness, Bruce thought of himself as a "good Christian." Even so, he had become complacent in his faith. His daily prayers felt automatic and he went to church more out of habit than for spiritual inspiration. The shift was subtle and he only really appreciated it in retrospect.

Bruce turned to his faith like never before when Lisa got sick. He began praying several times a day but rather than asking that "God's will be done," as he had been taught as a child, he prayed for a specific outcome: cure Lisa. As her suffering intensified, Bruce prayed more insistently and tried to strike deals with God. "Make my wife better and I'll never ask for anything else." When he and Lisa learned that she had only weeks to live, Bruce prayed for a miracle.

After Lisa died, Bruce questioned how an all-powerful and benevolent God could allow such a tragic thing to happen. Why had He not answered any of Bruce's pleas? Bruce's attitude hardened. He cursed God and bristled when friends or fellow parishioners offered platitudes such as "This is God's plan," "She's in a better place," and "Trust in Him."

Bruce's anger and skepticism did not soften overnight but, in time, he began to think more constructively about his relationship with God. One early realization stayed with him: he had never stopped believing that God existed. If he had not completely lost faith by now, he probably never would.

In time, Bruce gained a new perspective on the anger he had directed at God. He came to a simple conclusion: Lisa's death resulted from cancerous cells in her colon. Nothing more, nothing less. His initial instinct had been to blame someone or something but there was no obvious target. So, he had lashed out at the safest of all outlets for his rage and heartbreak.

Nearly two years after Lisa's death, Bruce was nominated by the leaders of his church to serve another term as an elder. He had to appear before the Council of Elders and answer questions about his faith. He had gone through the same process years earlier, when Lisa was healthy and life felt normal. He couldn't remember the answers he had given when the Council interviewed him for his first term, but he assumed that they were straightforward and conventional. This time was different.

Bruce spoke frankly to the Council about his spiritual struggles and how deeply his faith had been shaken. He was honest about his anger and confessed that sometimes he still wondered why God had not answered his prayers.

Bruce told the elders that despite his ongoing questions, he was more comfortable in his faith than ever before. Losing his wife had reshaped both his life and his connection with God. He explained that this relationship had come to resemble, in some ways, his other important relationships. It was complex, dynamic, and honest. His marriage with Lisa had included arguments and disappointments along with love and a deep connection. Now, his relationship with God had some of those same characteristics and that felt right to him.

Bruce's spiritual crisis mirrored a struggle that all the fathers went through. Naturally enough, each of the men had wanted to return to how things used to be. At times, they could not resist this pull and familiar ideas gave them temporary comfort. However, they also knew with certainty that life would never be the same. To grow, they had to rethink beliefs they had always taken for granted. There was no going back—only standing still or moving forward.

16

An Unexpected Partnership

Facilitating a support group and conducting group psychotherapy require similar skills. For both interventions, the leader encourages constructive interactions between group members in the service of psychological growth. However, there are important distinctions between these two types of groups that impact the relationship between the leader(s) and participants.

In group psychotherapy, traditional therapeutic rules apply: Patients receive mental health treatment for a diagnosed condition and are charged a fee for that care; the therapist and patients commit to maintaining the confidentiality of disclosures in the group; and records are kept for medical and legal purposes. In contrast, a support group is not considered formal psychotherapy. Consequently, less stringent rules apply.

This distinction influenced how we conducted the Single Fathers Due to Cancer support group. The men were not our patients and we were not their therapists. We were therefore able to partner with them in ways that would not have been possible otherwise.

From the beginning, a collaborative spirit defined our work with the fathers. The seeds of partnership were sown during the very first meeting when we welcomed their input and, in response to their feedback, altered both the structure and format of group meetings. In the months and years that followed, our partnership expanded and yielded unexpected benefits for us, the men, and countless other widowed fathers.

■

A quick search of the Internet or any bookstore reveals an abundance of resources for people grieving the loss of a loved one. However, there is remarkably little tailored specifically for widowed fathers. Researchers in the grief and bereavement fields have also largely neglected the challenges these men face. As our work with the fathers in the support group continued and intensified, we felt compelled to bring more attention to this underappreciated clinical need.

Our first instinct was to approach this subject academically and we drafted two manuscripts for professional journals. In the first paper, we aimed to raise awareness among our colleagues in the cancer and bereavement communities by highlighting the unique hardships of being a widowed father. The second paper described the formation of the support group and offered a blueprint for starting similar groups at other cancer centers.

When we mentioned the manuscripts to the fathers, they asked if they could read them. We emailed working drafts of both papers, but made it clear that we had no expectation that they would review or critique them. To our surprise, several fathers responded with substantive editorial suggestions that we incorporated into the final drafts. They were also grateful that we had understood their needs and done something to help other fathers like them.

In the United States alone, tens of thousands of men are raising children on their own after losing their spouses to cancer. We knew only seven of them. Before advocating for more support groups, we needed to learn about the experiences of widowed fathers on a larger scale. We assembled a research team of colleagues at the University of North Carolina and the National Institute of Mental Health in Bethesda, Maryland, and began designing a survey to test our clinical observations from the group.

Again, we turned to the true "experts" for guidance. We understood that asking the fathers for any input was not a trivial matter. Their schedules were already overloaded and we were hesitant to burden them further. Most importantly, we did not want them to see this request as a quid pro quo and made clear that our commitment to the support group was not contingent on their help with our research. Rather than ask for an immediate answer, we encouraged the men to think it over and said that we would revisit the topic at the next month's meeting. The men said that they didn't need that much time. They understood the value of their perspectives and appreciated the invitation. Over the next few months, each father helped us identify critical subject areas to explore in the survey and reviewed the wording of the questionnaire.

Ideally, we would have conducted detailed interviews with widowed fathers in person. However, we realized early on that identifying fathers to participate in the study would be a significant obstacle. There was no national advocacy organization for widowed fathers and no listserv or directory for us to access. We considered recruiting participants through cancer centers, but the fathers in our group reminded us that the hospital was the last place men in their situations wanted to go after their wives died.

With no practical means to locate widowed fathers, we concluded that an Internet-based survey would be the best way to reach them. But not many people will visit a website just to answer questions for thirty to forty minutes. During one group meeting, we asked the fathers what they thought about creating an online resource that would provide information for widowed fathers and host the survey.

Joe answered first: "You know, after Joy died, and before I met you guys, I felt like I was the only person in the world dealing with this. I knew that I wasn't, but I didn't know anyone else going through what I was. It would have been nice to find a website like this if for no other reason than to know that I wasn't alone."

"By now, we probably take this group for granted," Karl added. "We've been lucky to have had each other to meet with, talk to, and hear from every month. There's some guy living out in the middle of Idaho right now who just lost his spouse, trying to figure out how to raise his kids and going through all the same stuff as us. He doesn't have a support group to join but I can see how a website may help him get a handle on things."

By helping us create the website, the men saw another opportunity to help others. Over the ensuing months, we consulted them extensively. With their input, we included information on grief reactions, suggestions for communicating with children, and links to relevant resources.

When we started to write the Frequently Asked Questions (FAQ) page, we hit a snag. Generating questions was the easy part. The men had asked each other and us countless questions: "How can I tell if my kid is adjusting well?"; "Should we stay in the same house or move?"; "What do we do on Mother's Day; her birthday; our anniversary?"

The hard part was answering those questions. Each one had a seemingly endless array of "correct" responses, but answering every FAQ with some version of "it depends" was not going to be very useful. We needed to demonstrate that there were multiple ways to handle these situations so that a wide variety of fathers visiting the website could relate. We came up with an idea that would do just that but would again require the participation of the fathers in the group.

■

The men gathered in the usual conference room but not for a typical meeting and not at the usual time. On this Saturday afternoon, they would share their experiences as widowed fathers in recorded interviews for a much wider audience. One at a time, each man sat in a chair positioned in front of a large green screen as a videographer attached a small microphone to his shirt collar. Rather than talking with one another, the men answered a series of questions as they looked directly into the lens of a video camera.

Our solution to the FAQ dilemma was inspired by the diversity within our own group. By asking the same questions of each father, we elicited multiple answers. *What was most difficult for you after your wife died? How have you and your children coped with the first anniversary of your wife's death? When did you decide to remove your wedding ring? What was it like to date again?* The men answered honestly and poignantly. We had come to expect nothing less.

We worked with the videographer to edit the fathers' answers into a series of seven videos. Each clip was less than five minutes and provided several authentic and different responses to the same challenge. We gave each clip its own title: "The Fog of the First Few Months," "Going It Alone," "It's Been a Year Now," "The Wedding Ring Thing," and—borrowing the line that Bruce's friend used to snap him out of his first date panic—"Get Yourself Together, Man!"

Finally, in "Father to Father," the men offered advice that was direct, practical, and hopeful:

JOE: My message for Dads is to know that you're not going to get everything right. . . . You're going to make mistakes. Don't be afraid to make them. Don't be afraid to talk about things with your kids. Probably the most important thing is to really listen to them; really hear what they're saying.

DAN: When I feel the sadness coming on . . . or some memory brings back the flood of emotions, I take time to honor that. You can't just bottle it up. . . . One of the things that has helped me is that I've made a conscious effort to do the work of grief. That has really helped me get through some hard times.

KARL: I'd say this: Find other people who are in the same situation. If you can't find a support group like the one that we've put together here, then find somebody who has been through this. For me at least, having that shared experience and knowing that I was not the first person—or the only person—going through this was a big help. So, I think my first advice would be to find a support group or make your own of some kind.

BRUCE: The biggest thing that helped me was knowing that it does get better; knowing that as tough as it is right now—as deep as the pain is—as much as the grief hurts . . . in eighteen months, in two years, in two-and-a-half years, you will be able to see light again. You will be able to see happiness. You will be able to laugh. You will be able to enjoy friends. And you will learn how to re-create your life and build something new.

We launched the website under the domain name www.singlefathersdue-tocancer.org. As expected, the series of videos was the site's most popular feature. Widowed fathers all over the world could, for the first time, hear directly from their peers. We also hoped that fathers who found their way to the website would complete the survey.

In an effort to reach more fathers, we asked the UNC Communications Department to help us publicize the website. Several weeks later, they sent us the following email:

Don & Justin,
Good news! The TODAY Show is interested in doing a story on your group. They also want to interview one of the fathers. Do you think any of them would be willing?

The prospect of reaching a national audience was exciting, but we wondered whether any of the men would agree to be interviewed. Talking about their experiences as sole fathers for a video was one thing; broadcasting that pain on national television was another matter entirely.

Of all the men, Bruce had been the most public in sharing his grief. He had started a blog, spoken in front of his church congregation, and was writing a book about Lisa's illness and how it affected his family. When we asked him, Bruce was receptive and recognized immediately the potential to reach other fathers.

The next month, a film crew from NBC flew to North Carolina to tape a segment that would be broadcast the following month. They interviewed one of us (Don) for background on the group and then met with Bruce and his daughters at their home in Raleigh. He told them about Lisa, their marriage, and his struggles since her death. He described how he and his girls were finding their way and allowed the crew to film the four of them spending time at home.

The segment aired several weeks later. Both of us and every father in the group watched as the subject of widowed fatherhood received national attention for the first time. As expected, Bruce was outstanding and the piece captured the essence of what these men had endured.

A month after the *Today* show story, Jane Brody, a health columnist for the *New York Times*, reached out to us about our work with the support group. As a sixteen-year-old girl, Ms. Brody had lost her own mother to cancer and remembered vividly how her father and younger brother struggled in the years that followed. She interviewed Joe, Karl, and both of us for a beautifully written column that appeared in the Health section of the *New York Times*. Additional articles followed in local papers, and the Associated Press ran a piece on Father's Day. Importantly, each story explicitly mentioned the website and described it as a resource for widowed fathers. As a result, traffic to the site surged. On the day that the *Today* show piece aired, more people visited the site than during the previous six months combined. Similar traffic surges followed each subsequent exposure.

As the number of people who visited the website mounted, so did the number of widowed fathers who took the survey. In the end, four hundred and twenty-eight men completed a detailed questionnaire about their wives' end-of-life experiences and their own subsequent reactions. With the full partnership of the men in our group, we had collected the first and largest database about men who had lost a spouse to cancer and were raising children on their own. These data served as the basis for multiple manuscripts in professional journals and numerous presentations at cancer and bereavement conferences.

The final section of the survey included an open-ended question asking for feedback. We wanted to know whether the questionnaire touched on the right themes. What had we overlooked? Had the survey been too long? Was it too painful to complete? The responses were rich and insightful. More than anything else, we were astounded by their expressions of gratitude. One evening during a group meeting, we read a selection of the comments to the men.

> I liked watching the videos of men who talked about their loss, their feelings, what they did regarding whether or not to keep wearing their wedding rings, etc. It was helpful to hear that other men went through this, and to hear what they chose to do.

> It was like looking in the mirror.

> Keep doing what you're doing . . . it's helping a lot of single fathers out just by knowing we're not alone.

> It's been about eight months since my wife died of cancer, I think this will help.

> I am happy to find this site. I lost my wife to cancer and am raising my two children—10 and 6 years old. It is not easy but I need to find out from others how they coped.

> I'm very grateful to find this site. It is a great support, even from so far away.

> All I can say is that I wish you had been around when I lost my wife years ago. I participated in hospice counseling and spouse support groups, but no one else was confronting the same issues as I was as a single Dad with three young children.

Please, just keep on existing. There are times when sites and programs like yours are the difference between suicide and staying alive.

The men were gratified to hear that their work had such an impact on other fathers. They had joined the group for the benefit of their children and themselves. Along the way, they gave back and found meaning in helping others.

17

Hard-Earned Wisdom

n 1994, Kenneth Schwartz, a forty-year-old healthcare attorney from Boston, was diagnosed with advanced lung cancer. At different times during his progressive illness, he was deeply moved by aspects of his care that were less strictly medical or technical: a calming visit from a nurse prior to surgery; a personal connection with an anesthesiology resident from his neighborhood; and, toward the end of his life, the kindness and perspective provided by his oncologist.

Shortly before his death, Mr. Schwartz founded a non-profit organization to promote the kind of compassionate care that had meant so much to him. Two decades later, the Schwartz Center for Compassionate Healthcare reaches millions of patients and hundreds of thousands of caregivers to realize its founder's vision of more humane care for the seriously ill.

A cornerstone of the Center's work is the Schwartz Rounds program, which brings healthcare providers from multiple disciplines together for frank discussions about the emotional and psychosocial challenges of caring for patients. More than five hundred healthcare organizations around the world host these ongoing, non-traditional conferences.

A few years ago, the organizer of Schwartz Rounds at UNC invited us to lead an upcoming conference. She was aware of our work with the single fathers support group and wanted us to address the challenges that spouses face when caring for a partner with a terminal illness.

At the next group meeting, we mentioned this request to the men and asked them for their advice. Each father had been an eyewitness to the end of his wife's life and knew well how that heartbreaking time had impacted his entire family. Not surprisingly, they had a lot to say about end-of-life care and how it could be improved.

Karl was particularly passionate. "I've actually thought about this a lot since Susan died. Obviously, the patient is the focus, but I think it's also important for doctors to appreciate what the family goes through—especially when there are kids at home and the spouse is a co-parent. That dynamic alone influences so many things."

Then he made an unexpected offer. "If you guys think that the presentation would be more impactful if it came from one of us, I'd be willing to speak. Actually, I'd really like to do it."

The Schwartz Rounds organizer loved the idea and publicized the conference throughout our medical center with the title: "*Cancer Care: Through the Eyes of a Surviving Spouse.*"

The following month, Karl stood in the front of a room packed with oncologists, nurses, psychiatrists, psychologists, chaplains, social workers, and students from multiple disciplines. He eloquently described observations and feelings that he'd had during Susan's illness: the transition from partner to caregiver; tensions between him and Susan when they interpreted messages from her doctors differently; shifts in parenting and household responsibilities as Susan's health deteriorated; and the uncertainty of deciding when and how to tell his children that their mother was dying.

Karl prefaced his main message with an expression of gratitude to Susan's oncologist (who was in attendance) and her entire treatment team.

He thanked them for their thoughtfulness, compassion, and commitment to Susan even when it became clear that nothing more could have been done to treat her cancer. He had accepted that her disease was simply too aggressive.

But Karl, always the engineer, also saw room for improvement. He urged the providers in the room to help their patients have end-of-life conversations with those closest to them.

"For the most part, Susan and I avoided talking about her prognosis and all the 'what ifs.' As her husband, I didn't know how to start those conversations. Staying hopeful was important to Susan and that's what she asked me to do. So, I followed her lead. I told myself that it was *her* body, *her* treatment, *her* life—so what we did or didn't talk about was *her* decision.

"But there is so much that we never discussed and I regret that now. Susan and I needed one of the doctors, or someone, to sit us down, encourage us to have those difficult conversations, and give us some practical advice. I'm sure that's very hard for a lot of doctors to do and maybe some don't see it as their responsibility. But to me, that's an essential thing to do when someone is dying."

Sitting in the audience, we marveled at Karl's composure and the relevance of his message. He finished his presentation and answered one question after another for the remainder of the hour. At the end of the conference, our colleagues immediately formed a line to thank Karl personally. The Schwartz Rounds organizer subsequently told us that the evaluations of Karl's session were the best of the year.

Coincidentally, the conference occurred just a week before the anniversary of Susan's death. The men frequently struggled with these "anniversary reactions" so we emailed Karl to let him know that we were thinking of him. He replied with the following:

Guys,
Since our last meeting, I've been dreading the actual day far less. Doing that Schwartz Rounds really helped me. Maybe it was taking some action, maybe it was just the passage of time, maybe it was

actually going back to the hospital. But for whatever reason, I walked out feeling like a weight had come off my shoulders.

I still miss Susan, obviously, but when I've thought of her, I haven't had the tight feeling in my chest that I used to get. Maybe this is letting go—or moving on.

See you Monday,

Karl

That next Monday evening, Karl gave a confident report to the group. "What seemed to most deeply resonate with the audience was when I talked about how having conversations with Susan would have helped me adjust to being a widowed father." Perhaps more importantly for Karl, his Schwartz Rounds presentation proved to be a turning point in his grief.

■

Karl's presentation inspired us to continue working with the men in our group to reach more clinicians. Widowed parents have unique and rarely tapped perspectives on end-of-life care. Consequently, we decided to make an educational film for healthcare providers about these challenges. The uniformly positive responses to Karl's conference convinced us that the fathers would be compelling messengers. The Schwartz Center funded the production of the film and, once again, the group partnered with us enthusiastically.

We asked Russ and Bruce if we could interview them for the film since their wives' oncologists approached conversations about prognosis and end-of-life care so differently. Contrasting their experiences would allow us to emphasize the important role doctors can play in caring for families affected by advanced illnesses. We interviewed Russ and Bruce at their homes. The videographer also shot footage of their children around the house, playing basketball at the gym, and getting ready for school or church.

The two interviews were edited into a fourteen-minute film entitled *If I Should Not Return* that we presented at an annual conference of the American Psychosocial Oncology Society (APOS), a professional organization dedicated to the supportive care of patients with cancer. It was intended to be a "trigger film," that is, an emotionally evocative probe to stimulate discussion among physician trainees and healthcare providers. In alternating close-up shots, Russ and Bruce talk lovingly about their wives and feeling shocked that cancer had invaded their lives. Each father tears up as he talks about his wife's death and his children.

Later in the film, Russ and Bruce describe diametrically opposed interactions with their wives' oncologists. From the beginning, as Russ explained, Kelley's doctor stated clearly that her illness was fatal and that her time was limited.

"He told her that about six months is all she had. And almost to the day, she lasted six months."

Kelley and Russ metabolized that news together. Then Kelley got to work. She had specific ideas about how she wanted Russ to raise the boys and hoped that they would find ways to remember her after she was gone. Her oncologist was caring but forthright and that allowed Kelley and Russ to make concrete plans for their children.

Bruce and Lisa had neither that clarity nor that time. For the first five months of Lisa's treatment, there were no conversations about prognosis or end-of-life scenarios. In the film, as he did during the very first group meeting, Bruce described how this changed during a consultation with a new oncologist.

"Two weeks before she died, we got a second opinion. [The doctor] looked at all of our data and said 'your treatment … is very risky, but I don't see that you have any other options.'

"My wife asked, 'What does that mean?'

"He said, 'It means you could have weeks, maybe months.'

"That was *two weeks* before she died. And that was the first time I had heard that. Nobody else had told us that she was going to die.

"That conversation helped her realize that her time was short. She wrote me a note, she wrote to the girls, she got the summer schedules straight, and gave me all her passwords. But she was so sick, and so weak, and on so many drugs that her ability to shore things up in those last two weeks was very limited.

"My wife didn't get to tell my kids goodbye. That might have been very, very hard. But I probably would have liked for them to have that opportunity before she went into intensive care and couldn't speak anymore."

Lisa used that brief window as much as her body would allow but Bruce was left to wonder what else she could have done to prepare him and the girls if given more time. He understood that initiating those conversations could be extraordinarily difficult for physicians.

"Oncologists, and doctors in general, want to believe that they can heal you . . . and so want you to live. I mean, I think really they want that success story for you and for them. So, it's hard to face that reality. Rather than face it, [they] just avoid it. . . .

"Even in intensive care, the doctors said, 'She's responding.' I mean, she looked basically unconscious to me. And they said, 'Oh, she's responding; she's squeezing my hand.' And I thought that there was hope. There wasn't."

Bruce's message to clinicians echoed what Karl had conveyed during his presentation at Schwartz Rounds. He even volunteered a potential script for physicians:

> "We've seen miracles happen, and we have seen people recover. And that's what we're driving for. But you need to understand that this is very serious and you could have a limited amount of time. So, if there are things that you want to take care of . . . think about those things now."

"If I Should Not Return" was well received at the APOS conference. We uploaded the film to the website and encouraged colleagues at other cancer centers to use it for training purposes. At UNC, we continue to show it to medical students, residents, and oncology fellows in seminars on communicating difficult news and end-of-life care. Invariably, the film elicits rich interactions about both professional and personal experiences with terminal illnesses.

■

Our partnership with the men continued to shape our academic and clinical work in important ways. We remained committed to the needs of widowed fathers but also became increasingly interested in the end-of-life experiences of parents who are dying.

Under the leadership of Eliza Park, MD, a clinical investigator in our group at UNC, we launched a series of studies to better understand the supportive care needs of parents with advanced cancer. We learned that while medical decisions are often influenced by parental considerations, they are rarely discussed with health care providers. For mothers, in particular, worries about their family are ubiquitous and planning for their children's future is a top priority. We also found that despite agreeing on the importance of discussing these issues with each other, parents frequently struggle to initiate these difficult conversations on their own.

For me (Justin), what I learned from the fathers also transformed my work as a clinical psychologist. When I arrived at UNC, at about the same time as we started the support group, I expanded my clinical practice to provide psychotherapy to adults. Previously, I worked almost exclusively with children and adolescents, and spent several years as a pediatric psychologist at St. Jude Children's Research Hospital in Memphis, Tennessee. At St. Jude, I often counseled healthy parents with sick children. Once at UNC, I began to treat adults with cancer, many of whom also had children at home. For me, this was new clinical territory. I didn't realize it at the time but the fathers in the group had become my teachers in this regard.

One evening, I told the men about a patient in his late thirties, whom I had seen in psychotherapy. Paul had been diagnosed with pancreatic cancer the previous year and was told by his oncologist that his prognosis was very poor. In the midst of worsening pain and failing health, Paul was most concerned about his wife and two young children.

In therapy, Paul and I discussed his desire to help his children cope following his death. His wife joined us for two sessions which focused on their shifting parenting roles. He was also able to say clearly that he hoped she would re-marry one day. Those were exquisitely painful conversations. They were also the right ones to have.

Paul bravely addressed these issues in therapy but had not yet told either of his children that he was going to die. I empathized with Paul but encouraged him to talk with his children. Stories from the fathers in the group were helpful. I told him about Neill's son and how angry he was about not being told that his mother was going to die. I also described Bruce's continued regret that his girls never got to say goodbye to their mother.

Paul was clearly moved by these stories. "My kids are most important to me. I know that it's going to be really hard for them after I'm gone. So, I want to do what I can *now* to make things less difficult for them *later*. I'll talk with my wife about it."

Over the next several weeks, Paul found reasons to put off having "the talk." He knew that that he needed to tell them; he just kept waiting for the right time. Unfortunately, Paul's health was deteriorating rapidly and he was unlikely to live much longer.

My instinct was to press Paul. I described how Karl was once in a similar position and that he and Susan also put off those conversations, believing that there would be more time, a better time. But Susan's health and mental clarity failed more quickly than expected and those conversations never happened. I then shared with Paul what Karl had said at our very first group meeting: "It was too late before I realized it was too late."

The cautionary tale convinced Paul to act. Later that week, he and his wife sat down with their children and gently—but clearly—told them that their father was going to die. The conversation was as difficult as Paul had imagined it would be. But it allowed the children to begin saying goodbye to their father in a meaningful way.

"So, I want each of you guys to know," I told the group, "that's the kind of difference that you're making."

"Thanks for sharing that," Dan said. "We really appreciate hearing these things. It's nice to know that some good is coming from all this."

18

Winding Down

From the beginning the men had known, better than we did, that six sessions would not be enough. Changing the group to an open-ended format had been the right move, but we hadn't resolved the question of when the group should end. The fathers were clearly piecing their lives back together and the reasons for continuing to meet were becoming less clear.

As the group approached the three-year mark, attendance lagged. We wondered if it had run its course. One evening, we asked the men whether they wanted to keep meeting or if it was time to stop. We acknowledged that our work together had become increasingly collaborative but wanted them to know that they were not beholden to us. We never intended for the group to continue in perpetuity. Our focus had been to help them grieve and move forward. If they had reached that point, then they should to feel free to leave.

The fathers seemed surprised when we raised this topic. They quickly dismissed the idea that they felt obligated to remain in the group. Uncharacteristically, Russ spoke first, "I've never felt pressured. I come because it helps."

The topic of discussion during that session was whether it was time to stop meeting. Each father knew that he would eventually leave but up until that moment Steve's departure had been the only other occasion on which we discussed endings. Bruce reframed the issue: "Unless getting engaged and moving across state lines is the only ticket out the door, I guess we need to figure this out."

Karl approached the subject with his typical analytical style. "It sounds like there are two issues on the table. First, how does any one of us know when it's time to stop coming? For Steve, it was easy: He got married and moved away. For the rest of us, the decision comes down to whether coming here is still helpful. Obviously, each of us has to answer that for ourselves. The second question is whether it's time for the group as a whole to end. It seems to me that if enough of us decide that we don't need to come anymore, then there is no group.

"And there's something else that's worth us talking about. Is it possible that continuing to meet may actually be holding us back?"

"How do you mean?" asked Dan.

Karl explained his thinking. "Well, you could make the case that by staying in the group we're perpetuating a kind of a 'patient mindset'—like we *need* each other to get by. If we keep meeting, are we telling ourselves that we can't handle our situations on our own?"

"I don't think so," said Dan. "I can see your point, but I've never thought about it like that."

"I haven't either." Karl answered, quickly. "And I don't feel that way now. In fact, I'd like to keep meeting because I still find it helpful."

Neill reflected on when he first joined the group. "When I heard that it was called the *Single Fathers Due to Cancer* support group, the first thing that caught my attention was the word "cancer." I wasn't sure if I even qualified or would fit in since Deanna never had cancer. But I decided to give it a shot because two other words—*single* and *father*—captured perfectly who I was at the time. It wasn't just my circumstance. Being a widowed father was my entire identity back then.

"Both of those things are still true. But, more and more, I'm trying to think of myself in other ways. I have this new job, I'm trying to go out more with friends, and I've even been on a few dates. My life is still mostly shaped by being a single dad, but I'm trying to define myself as more than that.

"So, back to Karl's point, I can see how staying in a group just for men in our situation could make it harder to change how we view ourselves. Being a widowed father is probably not an identity that any of us wants to hold on to forever."

"Does that mean you think that it's time for you to stop coming?" Karl asked.

"No, no. I don't. In fact, I look forward to this night each month."

Joe spoke next. "I'll be honest. For whatever reason, I haven't given much thought to any of this. I'm sitting here thinking about it for the first time and I don't see how chatting with you guys for two hours a month is holding me back in any way. I'd say just the opposite."

He wondered aloud what it would take for him to leave the group. "It's hard to know. It's not as if I'm *over* Joy or anything. Just last month, I dropped my daughters off at college for the semester and couldn't stop thinking that Joy should have been with us. It still doesn't feel right. Next week is Grace's birthday, and I know that I'll feel the same way. There is no question that I'm doing a lot better than before. But if I keep getting torn up like this, maybe I do still need you guys."

As he often did, Bruce inserted some levity into the conversation. "Hold on, is that the criteria? Because if we keep meeting until we're no longer missing our wives, we'll be getting together until we're old men! I can see it now: courtesy vans from the retirement home bring us here each month; we shuffle in on walkers with those cutout tennis balls on the bottoms, and instead of feeding us subs, Don and Justin will order mashed potatoes and pudding. That's going to be one hell of a group!"

The table burst out in laughter. Joe joined in. "C'mon, Bruce, just think of all we'll have to talk about: the struggles and sorrows of being a single great-grandfather due to cancer." Moments like this one—when humor interrupted serious and complicated conversations—encapsulated the fathers' interactions and, more broadly, their relationships with each other.

Once the laughter subsided, Bruce returned to Joe's earlier point. "Seriously though, guys, we have to be fair to ourselves. We can't expect to not grieve anymore just because more time has gone by. *Of course* we still miss our wives! I don't expect that will ever stop. Just last week, I heard a song on the car radio and had to pull over because I was bawling. After a few minutes, I was fine and got back on the road. I expect things like that are going to keep happening from time to time. That doesn't mean I'm not doing okay."

Bruce then shared how this realization had crystallized for him a few months earlier while he was on a date. "We had gone out like four or five times. Nothing too serious, but it was going pretty well. We were talking after dinner and she just asked me, point blank, whether I was 'over' Lisa."

"Yikes. How'd you answer that one?" asked Joe.

"Well, I could understand where she was coming from. She was trying to figure out where she stood and if I was ready for a serious relationship. Still, I felt put on the spot and didn't have a good answer. I thought about it for a few seconds and tried to be honest. I told her: 'I think I'm as over Lisa as I'm ever going to be. But I will never be *completely* over her.' "

Bruce's words struck a chord with Dan. "I really like how you put that, Bruce. I think that's right. We don't need to beat ourselves up about still missing our wives. What matters is if it keeps us from moving forward."

Karl then put the question to Dan. "So, do you think we should stop meeting?"

"No, I'm not saying that," Dan answered. "You know, it's not just about our own grief, but also about our children, right? I know that all of our kids are still struggling and it's good to have this group to talk about that. So yeah, I'd like to keep meeting."

Karl scanned the table for the only vote yet to be cast. "Russ, what do you think?"

In his understated manner, Russ simply said, "I'm in."

The men wanted more time together and concluded that session with an explicit commitment to continue meeting. Yet their ambivalence was palpable. Debriefing later that evening, we both commented that whenever one of the men had hinted that the group may no longer be necessary, either he or another father immediately argued that the meetings needed to continue.

In the subsequent months, attendance picked up but the discussions had a noticeably different quality. The men engaged in less collective problem-solving, and instead shared more personal reflections about changes they had seen in themselves and each other. None of us fully appreciated it at the time, but the fathers were wrapping up the group in their own time and in their own way.

■

During one of the meetings shortly after the men decided to carry on, Dan mentioned for the first time that he played guitar and wrote songs as a hobby. He reached into his pocket, took out his smartphone and told the group there was something he wanted them to hear. He placed the phone on the table and played a recording of a song he had written about Sarah and his struggle to find peace after her death.

After the song ended, the room remained silent for a long moment before Bruce said: "That was great, man. Really nice."

Joe thanked Dan and asked for a favor. "Would you mind playing that last part again? That was pretty cool."

If I could have a word with you, the word might be change
I can't go back in time, but I can keep you on my mind.
Some things will never change
If I could have a word with you

It was a simple act; sharing something personal with trusted friends. But for Dan, it meant more than that. He had taken a risk and invited scrutiny in a way that would have been much more difficult a few years earlier.

■

Karl too had changed. When his former girlfriend had collapsed and was rushed to the hospital, it reminded him that life can be upended without warning. He broke off that relationship, in part, because he wasn't prepared to risk the stability he had worked so hard to restore for his family after Susan's death.

Sometime later, he met a woman named Allie. They had an instant chemistry and Karl enthusiastically told the men about this new relationship and why this time felt different. "There are a couple of things. First, my life is much more settled than before. I'm in a better place and less worried about trying to control everything. Second, I'm really crazy about Allie. For me, it was a matter of finding the right person at the right time."

When Karl subsequently announced his engagement, the other men were thrilled for him but not at all surprised. From the beginning, Karl had talked about Allie with an excitement the group had never seen in him. He knew that integrating his family with hers would be a major undertaking, precisely the kind of disruption in day-to-day life that he had tried to avoid since Susan died. But Karl was truly happy for the first time in years and he was all in.

■

Three years after Joy died, Joe finally checked off an item from his "90 Days to Me" plan and reorganized his home office. He took down Joy's plaques and awards from her days in the district attorney's office as well as most of the pictures of her that were scattered throughout the house. Next, he tackled the bedroom. The prospect of cleaning out Joy's side of the closet was daunting, so he asked one of her old friends for help. They went through each item and decided which ones to save for his daughters, which to donate to charity, and which ones to toss. In the end, he told the guys one night, it wasn't nearly as difficult as he had imagined.

Other things had also become easier. "I've pretty much got the morning routine down now," he said. "Making sure that Grace looks presentable for school and getting the kids out the door on time aren't really big deals anymore."

Work was also better. "I'm not just going through the motions for my job anymore. I used to justify that attitude by saying that I had a better 'perspective' on what was really important in life. Of course, that was bullshit. The truth was, my heart just wasn't in it. And then, as I often did during that time, I would get overly critical of myself.

"I really don't want that to be what's left over from that period of my life. I'm working on it and going easier on myself than I was a few years ago. Thankfully, I'm making progress on that front as well.

"So, guys, I'm happy to report that my 'give a shit' is back from the shop, and it's working again."

■

One evening, Bruce shared a story that, at first, sounded like yet another confession of parental failure. "Last week, I had a really busy day at work and totally forgot to pick up my daughter from play rehearsal after school. It just completely slipped my mind. When I checked my phone, there was this string of increasingly frantic texts: 'Dad, are you on your way yet?'; 'Seriously, where are you?'; 'DAD . . . WTH?!?!?' The last one was something like, 'Forget it! I called Grandma. Never mind!'

"I got home and my daughter started in on me right away. 'How could you forget about me? I had to stay at school a whole extra hour!' I apologized and explained that things got crazy at work. And then I told her to take a deep breath and relax. In the grand scheme of things, it was nothing more than a minor inconvenience. And I really meant it, too—I was sorry that I screwed up, but it just didn't impress me as that big a deal.

"But here's the thing. My response would have been so much different a couple of years ago. You guys remember when that teacher bought one of my kids a new pair of shoes because the ones she was wearing were so worn down? That completely crushed me. I felt like the worst father in the world. This time? I just wasn't that fazed. These aren't the things that really matter. I'm so much clearer about that now."

■

Of the seven fathers in the group, Russ was the last to start dating. He was sure that he had already found the love of his life and cancer had taken her away. That didn't stop those closest to Russ, including the men in the group, from encouraging him to be open to a new relationship. Eventually, he let a friend set him up with a woman named Darlene and their first date went well. On the way to the restaurant for their second date, Russ realized that he had forgotten his wallet at home and drove with her to get it.

He ran upstairs to grab his wallet and when he came back down Darlene was in the living room looking at the boys' "shrine" for their mother. Before Russ could say a word, she turned around and said that he needed to put away the pictures, and that it was not appropriate to have them up after all this time. Their date lasted another fifteen minutes, which was the time it took Russ to drive her home.

The evening reinforced Russ's sense that he wasn't ready and he reinstated his ban on dating. He maintained that he was content to focus on life with his sons. "It's just us now—the Three Musketeers—and we're doing just fine on our own."

One evening, many months later, Russ met a friend for dinner. Before long the conversation turned to a familiar topic. When his friend suggested that it was time for Russ to start dating again, Russ became defensive and insisted that he wasn't interested. But, on this night, his friend had a different idea. Without warning, he turned to a woman at the next table over, introduced himself and asked her if she was single. When she nodded her head, he said, "Great. I want you to meet my friend, Russ." He then stood up and abruptly excused himself.

Russ described his reaction during a group meeting. "Man, I was so mad to be sandbagged that way. I couldn't believe that my friend did that. But there wasn't much else I could do other than start talking with this woman. We actually ended up chatting for over an hour. It was crazy."

"Well . . . ?" Bruce asked. "Are you going to tell us the rest of the story?"

Russ grinned. "Her name is Kristen. We've been seeing each other a lot lately. She's, well . . . let's just say she's pretty special.

"It sounds ridiculous but I used to believe that there was just *one* right person out there for everyone and that I was lucky enough to have found my soul mate in Kelley. So, after she died, I didn't see any point in dating again. I figured that I'd already found my one person, and she was gone.

"I was wrong, though. There isn't just one person who you're destined to be with. That's been a really important change for me."

■

For three straight years, Neill and his children had continued their tradition of visiting Deanna's gravesite on the anniversary of her death and releasing balloons in her memory. Neill decided that for year four they would do something different. Go somewhere different. He took his family on a week-long cruise in the Caribbean the week before Thanksgiving.

The trip was precisely the family time Neill had hoped for. But when the anniversary date came at the end of the cruise, the crew told him and his children that they could not release balloons over the ocean for environmental reasons. Neill explained why this ritual was so important to his family, but the crew wouldn't budge.

So, he ran down to one of the ship's gift shops and bought all the soap bubbles he could find. Back on deck, he told his children that this year they were going to blow bubbles instead of releasing balloons. The modified ritual turned out to be a big hit. Neill stood beside his oldest daughter, Julie, as they watched the two youngest children laughing and chasing bubbles.

Neill choked up a little as he shared this story with the men in the group. Then he composed himself and said, "I can't help but think back to a few years ago. I walked in this room with no clue how to handle that first anniversary. I was so thankful to have you guys to turn to that night. But this time, I figured it out myself."

■

About six months after the group had considered, and then rejected, the idea of disbanding, attendance once again started to fall off. We emailed each father with a special request to make it to the next meeting. Everyone showed up and, for the second time, we asked them whether it was time to stop. The men had another honest and thoughtful discussion and concluded that the group had run its course.

This felt like the right decision to us as well. We told the men that working with them had been deeply meaningful to us and thanked them for showing

us the possibilities of reimagining life. The fathers expressed their appreciation for having been a part of something special and told us again that they
would be happy to help with any future projects, including this book.

For the first time in four years, the men would no longer be a regular
presence in each other's lives. They had forged an uncommon bond and
while they wished that they had not needed to meet in the first place,
they would be forever grateful that they had. In the parking lot after the
meeting, the men said their goodbyes. They gave each other a final round
of hugs and promised to keep in touch before getting in their cars and
driving home.

From the earliest stages of the single fathers project, we hoped that eventually groups like this would be offered at other cancer centers. We were convinced that the monthly, unstructured get-together contributed substantially to the men's healing. Each father told us that he felt the same way. But how would we know with confidence that this particular approach really makes a difference and should be replicated in a wider fashion?

We considered conducting a formal study to establish the effectiveness of the support group, but there would be several fundamental questions of scientific design to answer first. Should we compare a specific widowed father support group with a more general bereavement group? Would we restrict enrollment to men who had all lost their wives at roughly the same time? Should we try to enroll fathers with the same number of children or children of a similar age?

Perhaps most importantly, we would need to choose a principal outcome of interest. In other words, would we target a shorter duration of grief? A reduction in symptoms of depression? Improved parental competence? In the end, we decided that we were most interested in serving a larger number of widowed parents.

The original group came together in a natural way. Indeed, the fathers bonded with each other so quickly that after welcoming Russ and Steve, we decided to close membership rather than bring new members into such a close-knit group. However, newly widowed fathers continued to reach out to us. We needed to start another group.

Five fathers signed up for the second iteration of the group. We paid close attention to how the two groups compared with each other. Although the specific and heartbreaking details differed, the same general themes and challenges emerged in the second group. The men confronted the chaos of widowed parenthood, tried to help their children grieve while grieving themselves, and struggled to reimagine a future for themselves and their families.

During sessions with the new group, we frequently shared insights and advice that the original seven men had taught us. On countless occasions, we wished that the more recently bereaved fathers could hear directly from the "veteran" fathers. At the same time, potential group members continued to call us. Would we add a third group, a fourth? And would recently bereaved fathers have to wait for enough new members to launch another group?

We needed a new and more sustainable model and identified three objectives: (1) to streamline new member enrollment; (2) to integrate into the group the lived experience of veteran widowed fathers; and (3) to facilitate an individualized and thoughtful "off ramp" for those men ready to conclude their participation. We settled on running a single, ongoing group. We continue to meet monthly and men can join or leave at one of several times during the year.

New members are welcomed to the group during three designated meetings per year. Similarly, at three different meetings during each yearly cycle, fathers who are ready to leave the group can say good-bye in their own way. Thus, rather than prescribe the length of time a father needs to participate, the revised format allows for more flexibility and reflects the reality that some men benefit from longer (or shorter) involvement than others. For the other six meetings of the year, members neither join nor leave so that these important transitions do not dominate every session.

This approach makes the group available to new members every four months. Accepting new members into an established group allows for newly bereaved fathers to interact with men who are further removed from their spouses' deaths. These veteran fathers provide invaluable comfort and perspective to the recently bereaved men and also benefit personally from giving back in this way.

We still debrief after every meeting. The two of us compare notes, remind each other of particularly compelling interactions between the men, and ask ourselves a seemingly endless list of questions about this ongoing experiment: What is the active ingredient in this support group? Is it a sense of belonging, being understood and accepted, or the development of "groupness?" If so, what factors contribute to greater group cohesion?

We also wonder whether the cause of death makes a significant difference. Does it really matter if someone is grieving a spouse who died from cancer, heart disease, a car crash, or suicide?

Why limit the group to fathers? Would a mixed group of widowed fathers and mothers work just as well? We have no doubts that mothers would also benefit from participating in a gender-specific support group. But when we asked the original seven fathers how they would have reacted to a mixed-gender group, they all said either that they would have been less likely to join or that they would have been less likely to express their feelings so freely. In particular, the men said that they felt comfortable discussing insecurities about perceived parenting failures or issues related to dating precisely because they were among other men.

We also asked for their thoughts on including fathers who had lost a spouse or partner of the same sex. The men shared our view that the common denominator for participation in this group was being a widowed father and that any man facing these challenges would be welcomed.

In this same spirit, we recently expanded our research and educational efforts to reach both widowed mothers and fathers regardless of how their spouse or partner died. To reflect this broader scope of our work, the Single Fathers Due to Cancer website is now: www.widowedparent.org

■

In December 2016, in a support group meeting under the new format, a lovely father-to-father moment occurred. Two relatively new members of the group listened intently as one of the veteran fathers, Jerry, shared a message of patience and self-compassion.

When we first met Jerry, he was thirty-two and his wife, Sandy, had died from a glioblastoma, a highly aggressive brain tumor, just two months earlier. A short time before her diagnosis, they had moved with their three young children from Pennsylvania to North Carolina for Sandy's job. Sandy underwent two surgeries, chemotherapy, and months of physical and speech therapy before succumbing to her cancer. Shortly after her death, Jerry heard about our group from a church friend and asked if he could come to a meeting.

His first night in the group was painful for everyone in attendance. He began by telling us that he was almost unable to enter the building that night. It turned out that on the day Sandy died, she had had a seizure as Jerry was driving her to a clinic visit. He immediately pulled off the highway and ran into the nearest office building to call 911. That building happened to be the one where we hold our group meetings.

Despite this traumatic reminder of the worst night of his life, Jerry tried to continue with his story. Leaving his sandwich untouched, he cried, coughed, and struggled to even speak. But he made it through that first night and remained in the group.

Two and a half years later, now the most senior member of the group, Jerry spoke directly to two recently bereaved fathers who had just expressed how numb and overwhelmed they felt. "I was so much worse than either of you. I was sleeping four or five hours a night, felt like I was living an unreal version of my life, had a mortgage I couldn't afford, and was in fear of getting fired every day since I was barely showing up at work. Don and Justin will tell you, there were times I thought about suicide.

"But this does get better. You will find your way through this. It won't ever be completely okay again, but I'm here to tell you, you are not alone. The guys in this room understand. We've got your back."

One of the new fathers replied, "Right now, it's hard to see how this gets better." Then he went on, "I really hope you're right, so keep the advice coming."

As often happened, the meeting had run late and the fathers needed to get their kids home and into bed. We thanked the men and brought the session to an end.

"Great work, guys. See you all next month."

ACKNOWLEDGMENTS

We are deeply indebted to the seven fathers who participated in the original support group and trusted us to tell their stories. These men, together with the fathers who joined subsequent groups and completed our research study, gave so much of themselves to each other and to us.

The Single Fathers Due to Cancer project grew directly from our clinical work and would not have been possible without the creativity and dedication of our colleagues Eliza Park, Teresa Edwards, and Allison Deal from UNC and Barbara Biesecker from the National Institutes of Health. We are grateful to the Schwartz Center for Compassionate Care, Brian Stabler, Davis Stillson, Nic Beery, Steve Sallet, UNC CHAI Core, and Debra Morgan of WRAL-TV, for their generous contributions to the instructional film, video clips of the fathers, research survey, and website.

Several individuals helped us reach widowed fathers throughout the world. Jane Brody of the *New York Times*; Martha Waggoner of the Associated Press, and Stacey Naggiar from NBC's *Today* show all reported the fathers' story with journalistic integrity and great compassion.

The Dual Process Model of Bereavement was created by Margaret Schut and Henk Stroebe at Utrecht University in the Netherlands and provided us with an enormously helpful framework for our work with the fathers. We thank them for their elegant scholarship. Our colleagues Matthew Loscalzo, Franklin Miller, Jerry Schulman, Joan Rehm, Carole Geithner, and Deb Mayer reviewed early drafts of the book and provided us with invaluable guidance. The Chair of Psychiatry at UNC, David Rubinow, and the Director of UNC Cancer Care, Shelley Earp, have been inspirational mentors to us and supported this project from its inception. We are grateful to Robin Haring, Executive Assistant for the UNC Comprehensive Cancer Support Program, for her humor and uncanny capacity to squeeze time out of our schedules to work on this book.

The fathers would not have been able to attend group sessions unless they had someone to watch their children. We thank the UNC student-athletes who generously provided hundreds of hours of rambunctious childcare during our meetings.

As two first-time book authors, we've had a lot to learn. From the very beginning of this process, Andrea Knobloch from Oxford University Press understood what we wanted to accomplish and helped us make it happen. The editorial, publicity and marketing teams at Oxford, including Sarah Russo, Amy Whitmer, Erin Meehan, Tiffany Lu, and Josh Glickman, worked tirelessly to help us share the story of The Group. We were also very fortunate to stumble upon a brilliant literary agent, Jim Levine, and an extraordinarily gifted editor, Kathleen Kearns.

Our families and friends have been our greatest supporters. We hope that they know how much we appreciate their encouragement and insightful feedback on drafts of the book. We've received so much inspiration from our parents (Regina and Sheldon Rosenstein, Mary Ann Olsen and Ray Luce, Mike and Jan Yopp), children (Emma and Koby Rosenstein, Chloe and Gavin Yopp) and siblings (Byron Rosenstein, Robyn Silberstein, David Yopp). Finally, special thanks go to our wives, Mary Rosenstein and Colleen Yopp, for their love and endless patience.

American Psychological Association. (2013). *Diagnostic and statistical manual of mental disorders* (5th ed.). Arlington, VA: American Psychiatric Association.

Boelen, P. A., & Prigerson, H. G. (2012). Commentary on the inclusion of persistent complex bereavement-related disorder in *DSM-5*. *Death Studies*, 36, 771–794.

Boelen, P. A., & Prigerson, H. G. (2013). Prolonged grief disorder as a new diagnostic category in *DSM-5*. In M. Stroebe, H. Schut, and J. van den Bout (Eds.), *Complicated grief: Scientific foundations for health care professionals* (pp. 85–98). New York: Routledge/Taylor & Francis.

Bonanno, G. A. (2009). *The other side of sadness: What the new science of bereavement tells us about life after loss.* New York: Basic Books.

Breitbart, W. S., & Poppito S. R. (2014). *Meaning-centered group psychotherapy for patients with advanced cancer: A treatment manual.* New York: Oxford University Press.

Brody, J. (2013, April 23). A lifeline for widowed fathers. *New York Times*, pp. D4.

Calhoun, L. G., & Tedeschi, R. G. (2013). *Posttraumatic growth in clinical practice.* New York: Routledge/Taylor & Francis.

Check, D. K., Park, E. M., Reeder-Hayes, K. E., Mayer, D. K., Yopp, J. M., Rosenstein, D. L., et al. (2016). Concerns underlying treatment preferences of advanced cancer patients with children. *Psycho-Oncology*. Epub ahead of print. PMID: 27228327.

Frankl, V. (1964). *Man's search for meaning: An introduction to logotherapy.* London: Hodder and Stoughton.

Klass, D., Silverman, P. R., & Nickman, S. L. (1996). *Continuing bonds: New understandings of grief.* Washington, DC: Taylor & Francis.

Kübler-Ross, E. (1969). *On death and dying.* New York: Macmillan.

Ham, B. (2013). *Laughter, tears and braids: A father's journey through losing his wife to cancer.* Raleigh, NC: Author.

Mancini, A. D., Sinan, B., & Bonanno, G. A. (2015). Predictors of prolonged grief, resilience, and recovery among bereaved spouses. *Journal of Clinical Psychology*, 71 (12), 1245–1258.

Neimeyer, R. A. (2015). Reconstructing meaning in bereavement. In D. A. Winter & N. Reed (Eds.), *The Wiley handbook of personal construct psychology* (pp. 254–264). London: Wiley-Blackwell.

Park, E. M., Check, D. K., Song, M. K., Reeder-Hayes, K. E., Hanson, L. C., Yopp, J., et al. (2016). Parenting while living with advanced cancer: A qualitative study. *Palliative Medicine.* Epub ahead of print. PMID: 2748674.

Park, E. M., Check, D. K., Yopp, J. M., Deal, A. M., Edwards, T., & Rosenstein, D. L. (2015). An exploratory study of end-of-life prognostic communication needs as reported by widowed fathers due to cancer. *Psycho-Oncology*, 24, 1471–1476.

Park, E. M., Deal, A. M., Check, D. K., Hanson, L. C., Reeder-Hayes, K. E., Mayer, D. K., et al. (2016). Parenting concerns, quality of life, and psychological distress in patients with advanced cancer. *Psycho Oncology*, 25, 942–948.

Park, E. M., Deal, A. M., Yopp, J. M., Edwards, T., Stephenson, E. M., Hailey, C. E., et al. (2016, December 1). End-of-life parental communication priorities among bereaved fathers due to cancer. *Patient Education and Counseling.*

Park, E. M., Deal, A. M., Yopp, J. M., Edwards, T., Wilson, D. J., Hanson, L. C., et al. (2016). End-of-life experiences of mothers with advanced cancer: Perspectives of widowed fathers. *British Medical Journal of Supportive Palliative Care*, 6, 437–444.

Pelletier, D. (2013). *A word with you* [song]. Carrboro, NC: Writer.

Prigerson, H. G., Vanderwerker, L. C., & Maciejewski, P. K. (2008). A case for inclusion of prolonged grief disorder in *DSM-V*. In M. Stroebe, R. Hansson, H. Schut, & W. Stroebe (Eds.), *Handbook of bereavement research and practice: Advances in theory and intervention* (pp. 165–186). Washington, DC: American Psychological Association.

Rosenstein, D. L. (2008, April 27). Adapting to the possibilities of life. On J. Allison (Producer), *This I believe* [Radio program]. Louisville, KY: National Public Radio.

Rosenstein, D. L., Yopp, J. M., & Stabler, B. (Producers) & Stillson, D. (Director). (2013). *If I should not return* [Short film]. Chapel Hill, NC: Davis Stillson Associates.

Shear, M. K., Simon, N., Wall, M., Zisook, S., Neimeyer, R., Duan, N., et al. (2011). Complicated grief and related bereavement issues for *DSM-5*. *Depression & Anxiety*, 28, 103–117.

Snyderman, N. (2013, March 23). A safe place. *The today show* [Television broadcast]. New York: National Broadcasting Company.

Stroebe, M., & Schut, H. (1999). The dual process model of coping with bereavement: Rationale and description. *Omega: Journal of Death and Dying*, 26, 19–42.

Stroebe, M., & Schut, H. (2010). The dual process model of coping with bereavement: A decade on. *Omega: Journal of Death and Dying*, 61, 273–289.

Tedeschi, R. G., & Calhoun, L. G. (1996). The Posttraumatic Growth Inventory: Measuring the positive legacy of trauma. *Journal of Traumatic Stress*, 9, 455–472.

Waggoner, M. (2013, June 15). Dads whose wives died of cancer turn to NC group. *Associated Press.*

Wainwright, L. (1969, November 21). A lesson for the living: A young leukemia patient talks to a seminar. *LIFE*, 67(23), 36–43.

Wakefield, J. C. (2012). Should prolonged grief be reclassified as a mental disorder in *DSM-5*? *Journal of Nervous and Mental Disease*, 200, 499–511.

Wakefield, J. C. (2013). The *DSM-5* debate over the bereavement exclusion: Psychiatric diagnosis and the future of empirically supported treatment. *Clinical Psychology, 33,* 825–845.

Winnicott, D. (1992). *The child, the family and the outside world.* London: Pelican Books.

Yopp, J. M., Park, E. M., Edwards, T., Deal, A. M., & Rosenstein D. L. (2015). Overlooked and underserved: Widowed fathers with dependent-age children. *Palliative & Support Care, 13,* 1325–1334.

Yopp, J. M., & Rosenstein D. L. (2013). A support group for fathers whose partners died from cancer. *Clinical Journal of Oncology Nursing, 17,* 169–173.

Yopp, J. M. & Rosenstein D. L. (2012). Single fatherhood due to cancer. *Psycho-Oncology, 21,* 1362–1366.

Zisook, S., Corruble, E., Duan, N., Iglewicz, A., Karam, E. G., Lanuoette, N., et al. (2011). The bereavement exclusion and *DSM-5. Depression & Anxiety, 29,* 425–443.